WINNING VIRTUES

Success Principles of Kingdom Champions

AYORINDE IDOWU

WINNING VIRTUES
Success Principles of Kingdom Champions

Copyright © 2018 by **Ayorinde Idowu**

ISBN: 978-1-944652-83-8

Printed in the United States of America. All rights reserved solely by the publisher. This book or parts thereof may not be reproduced in any form, stored in a retrieval system, or transmitted in any form by any means - electronic, mechanical, photocopy. Unless otherwise noted, Bible quotations are taken from the Holy Bible, New King James Version. Copyright 1982 by Thomas Nelson, Inc., publishers. Used by permission.

Published By:
Cornerstone Publishing
A division of Cornerstone Creativity Group LLC
Info@thecornerstonepublishers.com
www.thecornerstonepublishers.com

Author's Information
To contact the author or to order copies of the book, please call (281)-989-2208 or E-Mail: Ayorinde_idowu@hotmail.com

CONTENTS

Dedication..7

Acknowledgments...9

Introduction..11

Chapter 1
Be Courageous..13

Chapter 2
Sow The Word, Reap Wonders..................................37

Chapter 3
Persevere To Prevail..53

Chapter 4
Master Your Mind...67

Chapter 5
Examine Your Loyalty...81

Chapter 6
Your Refuge In A Restless World...............................91

Chapter 7
Patience Is Still Golden...107

Chapter 8
Hearing The Voice Of God..................................117

Chapter 9
Knowledge Is Power..129

Chapter 10
Take Time To Be Holy...145

Chapter 11
Dominion Over Sickness.....................................161

Chapter 12
Finding True Happiness......................................175

Concluding Notes...190
About Ayorinde Idowu..191
References..192

DEDICATION

To all my grandchildren.

Hallelujah!

ACKNOWLEDGMENTS

Many thanks from the bottom of my heart to the following great people in my life for the support, encouragement, and inspirational motivation received from them that fueled the writing of this book: Pastor Dave and Pastor (Mrs.) Eunice Arogbonlo, The Rt Rev Dr. Titus B. Olayinka, my darling wife, Mildred Idowu and my entire family over here in Houston, Texas.

My gratitude also to Pastor Gbenga Showunmi, and Mr. Ola Aboderin for their professional assistance at Cornerstone Publishing Group.

INTRODUCTION

One striking observation I have made while studying the lives of trailblazers and highflyers in the various fields of human endeavors is that reaching and flourishing on the pinnacle of success goes beyond merely being talented or ambitious. There is a combination of principles and character traits that give wings to talent and direction to ambition. It is lack of this basic understanding that has made many gifted and energetic individuals whom the world had considered very promising and destined for greatness to suddenly crash out and end their dreams (and sometimes their lives) in defeat and disgrace.

The same applies to the Christian race and the Kingdom life in general. The difference between champions and failures, fruit-bearers and time-wasters, culture-changers and compromisers is often not just the amount of zeal that each possesses, but the degree of knowledge obtained and the extent of commitment to the application of such knowledge. Indeed, this was why Paul lamented about his religious brethren, saying that they demonstrated so much zeal but not according to knowledge (Romans 10:1-3). And it was for the same reason that he wrote to the Corinthians, reminding them that not all who run in a race obtain the victor's prize, and charging them to run like those who really wished to win (1 Corinthians 9:24).

I congratulate you if you have received Christ into your life and become a member of God's family and Kingdom. But you must know that you have not just come into the Kingdom to stay; you have been brought in to thrive, to grow, to prosper, to progress, to reproduce and, by so doing, continually bring glory to God. The secrets of achieving these Kingdom goals and more are what you will find in this book.

Even if, from all indications, you are presently doing well in the Kingdom, I assure you that there are much higher heights to attain and greater victories to obtain. I implore you to prayerfully go through the pages of this book and you will discover greater riches and joys in Christ Jesus that are meant for you!

CHAPTER 1

BE COURAGEOUS

I would define true courage to be a perfect sensibility of the measure of danger, and a mental willingness to endure it. —W.T. Sherman

Welcome aboard the flight of champions! Our destination point is the pinnacle of greatness, which is marked by Christ-like virtues, all-inclusive dominion, destiny-impacting accomplishments and unlimited joys of fulfillment!

As we proceed on our flight, we will have to halt, here and there, to view certain landmarks that have been left for us by those who have gone before us. These landmarks constitute the chapters of this book. And since it is expected of us to learn from these landmarks and deploy the lessons to our advantage, it is fitting that I begin with a clarion call to courage.

Why the call to courage? We need courage to not only steadfastly imbibe and demonstrate the various virtues that we will be exposed to at these different landmarks but also because courage appears to be the most critical virtue missing in the world today, leading to the seeming triumph of evil, despair and hopelessness that we witness all around us.

What then is courage? Courage is another word for *"fortitude", "strength", or "bravery"*. It involves undertaking courageous tasks that can be audacious, gallant, and daunting; therefore, it is a crucial Christian virtue. It is one of the four inherent or fundamental virtues, which comprise wisdom, courage, temperance, and justice (Philippians 4:8).

Courage is a virtue that enables us to act despite our fears. It helps us to do the right thing, regardless of criticisms and oppositions. As Eddie Rickenbacker says, "Courage is doing what you're afraid to do. There can be no courage unless you're scared." Courage does not make us act pointlessly, but for a great good that we perceive through hope to be attainable.

For the believer in particular, demonstrating the virtue of courage involves taking a difficult or an unpopular stance, despite pressures to compromise; or sometimes undertaking dangerous tasks for the sake of obeying God's word, doing God's will, defending the gospel, advancing God's Kingdom or seeking the welfare of other people. Essentially, it is the quality of being able to do the right under difficult circumstances.

EXEMPLARS OF COURAGE

Let me give you a good example here to illustrate what courage for the believer entails. The famed Prussian king, Frederick the Great, was a known agnostic. However, one of his most trusted officers, General Von Zealand, was a devout Christian. During a certain festive gathering, the king wanted to introduce some humor to the occasion, and so began making crude jokes about Christ. Everyone laughed at the king's comments – except Von Zealand.

Finally, the General arose and addressed the king: "Sire, you know I have not feared death. I have fought and won 38 battles for you. I am an old man; I shall soon have to go into the presence of One greater than you, the mighty God who saved me from my sin, the Lord Jesus Christ whom you are blaspheming. I salute you, sire, as an old man who loves his Savior, on the edge of eternity."

Eyewitnesses reported that as the fearless believer spoke, the place went silent, as the rebuke pierced the hearts of the people. And with a trembling voice the king replied, "General Von Zealand--I beg your pardon! I beg your pardon!" With that, the party quietly ended.

This contemporary example resonates with several others in the Scripture. Whether it is Jesus denouncing the religious leaders for their hypocrisy, or David facing Goliath, or Elijah standing before Ahab to declare God's judgment, or Esther going before the king to plead for the preservation of her people, or Daniel refusing to be silenced, or the three Hebrew children daring Nebuchadnezzar or John the Baptist rebuking Herod, or Paul before Felix and Agrippa – there are so many cases that exemplify what true courage means and what God requires of us as end-time believers.

PERSONAL DEMONSTRATIONS OF COURAGE

I turned 70 years old recently and in the course of my reflections, I recalled some instances in which I was empowered by God to demonstrate courage, even when I didn't really know what I was doing. I recall, for instance, that after my high school graduation in 1963, I had opted to major in the sciences, despite not having had an opportunity to read any science subject because the high school I attended had been unable to afford science facilities. However, because I was passionately determined to become a scientist, I found a solution to make up for the five-year science deficiency from my former handicapped local government school system.

I suddenly discovered that there was a remedial post-high school institution designed to cater for students that needed to make up for deficiencies in science. It was a preliminary one-year crash program to gaining admission to the university. It was a very complex transitional period for me because of financial constraints in my family, and the fact that I had to move out of the suburban town of Ogbomoso in Western Nigeria to live in Lagos, where my new school was located.

The city of Lagos was the Federal Capital of Nigeria as at then. It was densely populated, chaotic, and with a high cost of living. I had to live with my cousin who shared a one-room, stand-alone habitation. I happened to be the only male of seven siblings in my family, and it was the very first time that I ever moved out of my hometown to live outside. It was a very difficult decision for my family, but I prepared to bravely cope with any challenge that would come with my Lagos sojourn. The rest is history as I eventually passed the final examinations in all the preliminary science subjects, and gained admission to an American University to major in Geology in 1970.

Travelling out of Nigeria to the US in the 1970 was also a major decision for me – and I consider it a step of faith and courage, given the prevailing circumstances then. Finance was a major challenge, as I had just about $200 in my wallet when I landed in Chicago, Illinois, in August, 1970. My slim hope was to stay with a high school friend who had left Nigeria to Chicago less than two years earlier and shared a two-bedroom flat with another friend.

This friend of mine purchased my flight ticket on credit terms with a minimum deposit of $100 and mailed it to me in Nigeria to use for my travel to the US. The game plan was that I would join him in Chicago and work to first offset the cost of the ticket as soon as I arrived. There were so many other challenges involved in this arrangement, but I was always aiming for the end product – a university degree in Science in an American university. Again, the rest is history, and my dreams surely became true! Glory to God for the grace!

I vividly recall also my first technical paper presentation abroad. This was in 1997, while I worked as a geologist/geophysicist for the Nigerian National Petroleum Corporation (NNPC) in Lagos, Nigeria. As chief geologist, I participated in various oil and gas exploration development and production economics in the Niger Delta basin with our joint venture (JV) partners. This was at the beginning of marginal oil fields development in Nigeria. I came up with an abstract and proposal for a technical paper presentation on marginal oil field production economics and feasibility, based on the Nigerian government fiscal terms.

The paper was rightly timed, as the world's oil producing companies were then focused on enhancing oil recovery feasibilities and techniques. My paper proposal was quickly accepted and I was invited by the American Association of Petroleum Geologists (AAPG) to present it at the North Pacific Conference, held in Honolulu, Hawaii. I had presented technical papers in my company and within Nigeria on a smaller scale, but this was unique in that it was going to be my first international presentation outside Nigeria.

At the start of my preparation and research on the paper, which was titled "Marginal Oil Field Development and Economics in Nigeria", I was not so self-conscious as I later became. The paper was to cover the entire facet of oil exploration, development and production economics, which was a comprehensive test of my proficiency in not just one branch of the oil field profitability, but expertise in oil and gas technology, involving professionals such as geologists, geophysicists, petroleum engineers, mechanical engineers, accountants and economists. The presentation was to be made at a forum consisting of various experts from different parts of the world, as well as CEOs of multinational oil and gas companies. It was to provide an avenue for CEOs, shareholders, and investors to personally witness the feasibility of marginal oil field economics in Nigeria.

Honestly, I became nervous and bothered, as soon as I realized the global scope of the forum and the accuracy and proficiency that such an international presentation demanded. The world's oil industry family was waiting for facts and figures that accurately defined the feasibility of marginal oil fields development in Nigeria. I began to imagine the enormity of my presentation, and how my integrity and professional competence would be put to the test in front of such a professional gathering of company executives.

I happened to be basically a geologist, but had now been seriously challenged to deal with the engineering, accounting, economical, and administrative aspects of an oil field. Initially, I was disturbed, but I was determined to be successful, as I considered it a great opportunity to advertise my professionalism and that I just must deliver the great expectations.

The strategy of my preparation focused on discussions and interactions with various professionals in my company and other similar oil organizations in the city. Specifically, I interviewed a few guys who were involved in such a worldwide scale of technical presentations. The preparation thus became simplified and I was eager to get to Honolulu to make my presentation.

I recall that the best advice that helped me was that I should focus on the materials and the interpretation of my dataset, and not the statuses and cadres of the professionals present.

When the day for the presentation eventually came, all my fears had been banished. I became emboldened, being my own research project. I courageously had a great success!

CATALYSTS OF COURAGE

From my experience and those of others that I have mentioned, you can develop and demonstrate courage in all situations by learning the following secrets:

1. Prioritize God's word above physical circumstances and appearances: 2 Corinthians 5:7 says, "For we walk by faith, not by sight." The life of the conquering believer is a life governed by faith in God's unchanging faithfulness to His word, amidst the uncertainties and limitations that characterize life on earth. Check out the roll call of great men and women who earned commendation from God as overcomers over the battles of life in Hebrews 11. You will find that they were people who esteemed and held on to God's word, regardless of the things they faced, heard or saw. To them, the daily watchword for living was "Let God be TRUE and let all others – people, circumstances, negative reports, gloomy forecasts, disturbing dreams, scary prophecies, discouraging comments etc. – be

LIARS!" Let this be your watchword too. Accept, believe and meditate only on God's word, not on what circumstances or people want you to believe.

2. Be aware that cowards will not make heaven: This may surprise you but it is nonetheless true and scriptural. One of the forces that prevent people from fulfilling their destinies on earth and making it to heaven at last is fear or cowardice. Revelation 21:8 says, "But the cowardly, unbelieving, abominable, murderers, sexually immoral, sorcerers, idolaters, and all liars shall have their part in the lake which burns with fire and brimstone, which is the second death."

Fear often prevents people from doing the right and pushes them into doing the wrong. The reason many find it difficult to heed the call to salvation or remain steadfast in the will of God is because of fear of men, persecution and alienation. This is why you should earnestly resist fear and choose to be courageous in doing the right at all times. God exhorted Joshua in Joshua 1:6-7, "Be strong and of good courage, for to this people you shall divide as an inheritance the land which I swore to their fathers to give them. Only be strong and very courageous, that you may observe to do according to all the law which Moses My servant commanded you; do not turn from it to the right hand or to the left, that you may prosper wherever you go."

God had to give Joshua this admonition because He knows that none can truly stand in righteousness, obey His commandment and overcome the pressures from Satan and his agents without personal conviction and courage. This was why the same command was severally given to the Israelites, as they journeyed to possess the Promised Land. (see Deuteronomy 31:6, for instance). Unfortunately, many could still not enter God's rest because of fear and unbelief (Hebrews 3:19).

In many other instances in the Scripture where great undertakings were to be embarked upon, we find the same call to courage and steadfastness because without courage, failure is inevitable. David gave this charge to Solomon when he was to build the temple (1 Chronicles 28:20). Similarly, King Hezekiah encouraged his subjects to withstand the enemy's siege (2 Chronicles 32:6-8); while Joshua gave his own charge to Israel to fight (Joshua 10:25).

3. Fear no man but God: Proverbs 29:25 says, "The fear of man brings a snare, But whoever trusts in the Lord shall be safe." A man may command your admiration, honor and respect, but never your fear. God is the ultimate judge of our actions and intentions; thus He alone should take the primary place in all our considerations. We do only what He approves and reject whatever He disapproves, regardless of what any man says or thinks. When we allow the fear of man to dominate our hearts, we naturally ensnare and enslave ourselves.

A snare can be fatal (Proverbs 13:14; 14:27; 18:7). Fear is translated literally *"sheer terror"* (1 Samuel 14:15; Isaiah 4:4; Daniel 10:7). For these reasons, a wise person does not fear the mortal man. The One to fear is the Lord, who is both able to protect and to destroy (Proverbs 18:10; Luke 12:4-5).

4. You have to be dead to self and alive to God: This is the first command in the Book of Romans. Romans 6:11 says, "Likewise you also, reckon yourselves to be dead indeed to sin, but alive to God in Christ Jesus our Lord." To reckon yourself dead to something is to take your mind off its consciousness. To live a life of courage, you must be dead to the consciousness of your own weaknesses and limitations and focus on the infinite strength and omnipotence of the Spirit of God that lives inside of you. This is why Paul the Apostle says, "I can do all things through Christ who strengthens me" (Philippians 4:13). It was the same admonition that Zechariah was asked to deliver to Zerubbabel. "So he answered and said to me: "This is the word of the Lord to Zerubbabel: Not by might nor by power, but by My Spirit,' Says the Lord of hosts. 'Who are you, O great mountain? Before Zerubbabel you shall become a plain!" (Zechariah 4:67).

So, it's not by our natural skills, talents, connection or experience; it's by the help of God's unconquerable Spirit that we accomplish all that we have been assigned to accomplish. Therefore, whatever instruction or commission you have received from the Lord, or whatever challenge you have to deal with, look away from yourself and focus on GOD alone. "Look to Me, and be saved…For I am God, and there is no other" (Isaiah 45:22).

5. Know that you have got only one life: Since you have only one life to live, be determined to use it for the glory of God alone. 1 Corinthians 3:16-17 says, "Do you not know that you are the temple of God and that the Spirit of God dwells in you? If anyone defiles the temple of God, God will destroy him. For the temple of God is holy, which temple you are."

The Corinthians were called by Apostle Paul to have self-awareness about the ultimate identity of their corporate body. They were a temple built by God; therefore, they were required to honor God with their body, as anyone who defiles God's temple will, as recompense, be destroyed by God.

DIMENSIONS OF COURAGE

There are different ways and different areas of our lives in which God requires us to demonstrate courage.

His grace is available to fill us with the following dimensions of courage:

1. Courage for obedience: This is the courage to obey and do the will of God, regardless of circumstances. The greatest act of courage was Christ's obedient death on the cross which reveals Him as the ultimate selfless role model. Matthew 26:39-42 says of Him, "He went a little farther and fell on His face, and prayed, saying, "O My Father, if it is possible, let this cup pass from Me; nevertheless, not as I will, but as You will." Then He came to the disciples and found them sleeping, and said to Peter, "What! Could you not watch with Me one hour? Watch and pray, lest you enter into temptation. The spirit indeed is willing, but the flesh is weak." Again, a second time, He went away and prayed, saying, "O My Father, if this cup cannot pass away from Me unless I drink it, Your will be done."

The cup that Jesus refers to was God's wrath against sin. With the words "if it is possible, let this cup pass", Jesus wished His Father could provide forgiveness by some other means other than His sacrificial death. He knew that God's power could make it possible for Him to evade the power of the Jewish and Roman executioners (Matthew 26:53), but He did not want to reject His Father's plan to provide salvation for the world.

This is an exemplary demonstration of courage lived out in obedience to God's holy demand, and for the ultimate welfare of lost sinners. Courage is, therefore, not foolhardiness and reckless abandon; rather it aims at God's holiness and the welfare of others, with a full realization of both the actual and potential danger and cost involved.

2. Courage for conquest: This is the courage to confront and conquer difficulties with divine strength. A clear instance of this is the encounter between David and Goliath. That encounter with Goliath demonstrates the dauntless courage of youth, the bragging of a terrible giant, and the defeat of a seemingly unstoppable warrior by means of a mere simple weapon, powered by divine grace. It is the story of a hero who wins through the strength of his faith in the Almighty God. 1 Samuel 17:45-48 says, "Then David said to the Philistine, "You come to me with a sword, with a spear, and with a javelin. But I come to you in the name of the Lord of hosts, the God of the armies of Israel, whom you have defied. This day the Lord will deliver you into my hand, and I will strike you and take your head from you. And this day I will give the carcasses of the camp of the Philistines to the birds of the air and the wild beasts of the earth, that all the earth may know that there is a God in Israel. Then all this assembly shall know that the Lord does not save with sword and spear; for the battle is the Lord's, and He will give you into our hands."

David's declaration to Goliath highlights the contrast in battle strategy. The Philistine relied on sword, spear and javelin, but David fought in the name of (as the representative of and with the authority of) the Lord of hosts. David insisted that when victory was his, all the world would know that Israel had a God mighty enough to rescue in seemingly impossible situations.

3. Courage for Kingdom exploits: Prior to the coming of the Holy Spirit, with great power and boldness, on the disciples, Peter had a lot of bravado, a false and untested courage. Consequently, he ended up denying thrice that he ever knew Jesus, due to perceived threat to his life.

However, shortly after the coming of the Holy Spirit (as promised by Christ in Acts 1:8), Peter, after his initial failure of courage, showed an incredible, new strength. Rather than hide away when the apostles were being mocked by witnesses and bystanders, he declared God's word boldly, winning multitudes to the Kingdom (Acts 2:1-41).

From that moment on, Peter's life would never be the same again. Indeed, by his fruitful growth in the faith, he proclaimed his faith in Jesus more publicly. Even after being beaten and imprisoned, he went right back into preaching in the public again (Acts 5:17-42). His life eventually ended in willing martyrdom in Rome rather than deny his Lord, while the Holy Spirit encouraged him in the face of evil. No wonder he could write in 2 Peter 1:3-8, "as His divine power has given to us all things that pertain to life and godliness, through the knowledge of Him who called us by glory and virtue, by which have been given to us exceedingly great and precious promises, that through these you may be partakers of the divine nature, having escaped the corruption that is in the world through lust. But also for this very reason, giving all diligence, add to your faith virtue, to virtue knowledge, to knowledge self-control, to self-control perseverance, to perseverance godliness, to godliness brotherly kindness, and to brotherly kindness love. For if these things are yours and abound, you will be neither barren nor unfruitful in the knowledge of our Lord Jesus Christ."

The example of Joshua too is significant here. His initial deposition also involved a lot of fear when he was suddenly asked by God to take over the leadership of Israel after the death of Moses. He hesitated before going across the Jordan into the Promised Land. He also nursed some other fears, which the all-knowing God was fully aware of. This was why He told him, "No man shall be able to stand before you all the days of your life; as I was with Moses, so I will be with you. I will not leave you nor forsake you. Be strong and of good courage, for to this people you shall divide as an inheritance the land which I swore to their fathers to give them. ...Have I not commanded you? Be strong and of good courage; do not be afraid, nor be dismayed, for the Lord your God is with you wherever you go" (Joshua 1:5-9).

The *"frame"* of God's promised presence in the above passage indicates that Joshua's success would come because God was with him. Joshua became emboldened after God repeatedly told him three times to have courage. He was fully aware that God does not speak without a purpose, nor does He lie or fail.

4. Courage for uprightness: This is the courage to maintain holy living, regardless of prevailing practices and pressures. Society has set new standards in attitudes towards authority, modesty, and the sanctity of marriage, while we watch the world pursue the path to destruction. With current world's trends, we cannot but ask why we are here "for such a time as this". Of course, there is something we can do as individuals to remain faithful and help others understand God's will in their lives. This involves preaching the gospel and discipleship.

Queen Esther was encouraged by her uncle, Mordecai, to approach the king for favor in order to deliver the Jews from the threat of mass destruction being concocted by Haman. Mordecai told Esther: "Do not think in your heart that you will escape in the king's palace any more than all the other Jews. For if you remain completely silent at this time, relief and deliverance will arise for the Jews from another place, but you and your father's house will perish. Yet who knows whether you have come to the kingdom for such a time as this?" (Esther 4:13-14).

Mordecai's charge to Esther was direct and to the point, as Esther had no self-choices. Appearing unbidden before the king could mean death, but remaining silent, when so many servants and eunuchs knew of her connections to Mordecai, the Jew, could likewise result in her death, once the genocide was carried out.

Mordecai and Esther would regard relief and deliverance, whatever the source, as attributable ultimately to God's providential care for His people. This conclusion is supported by Mordecai's famous suggestion that Esther had "come to the kingdom for such a time at this." This meant God had a destiny for Esther. All the various but coherent events in the last four years apparently put her in this position for this very moment.

Other gallant displays of courage for uprightness include that of Joseph, who boldly told Potiphar's wife who had tried to seduce him into having an immoral relationship with her, "How then can I do this great wickedness, and sin against God?" (Genesis 39:9). Daniel also was thrown into the den of lions after daring the king in defiance of his decree to worship the graven idol. Daniel knew the consequences of praying to God as against the king's decree; yet he had the courage to do what was right. He did not attempt to hide his faith (Daniel 6:10).

5. Courage for steadfastness in trials: This is courage to withstand trials and buffeting from the enemy, without compromising or losing the faith. Paul, in Ephesians 6:10-13, exhorts, "Finally, my brethren, be strong in the Lord and in the power of His might. Put on the whole armor of God, that you may be able to stand against the wiles of the devil. For we do not wrestle against flesh and blood, but against principalities, against powers, against the rulers of the darkness of this age, against spiritual hosts of wickedness in the heavenly places. Therefore take up the whole armor of God, that you may be able to withstand in the evil day, and having done all, to stand."

Three times Paul calls for believers to stand against the devil's schemes (Ephesians 6: 11, 13, 14). He encourages us to be strong, putting on the whole armor of God – reminding us of the shield of faith, the helmet of salvation (that is, our hope of eternal life), of the power of truth, and of righteous living. These elements give us confidence and bravery, as well as encouraging us to fulfill God's purpose for our lives.

LESSONS FROM THE COURAGEOUS

From all we have considered so far, the following nuggets of truth stand out for our benefit:

1. All the heroes of our faith in the Scripture and in recent times are courageous people. They did what they were instructed to do, in spite of their fears and the risks involved. We too must learn to accomplish our God-given tasks, no matter how risky and how big our fear appears to be. Simply put, courage is: "do it while you are afraid."

2. Every divine assignment will always seem too big for the natural man, and until we step out in faith, we will not discover the awesome wonder God has in store – just as it was with Moses, Gideon, Esther and the likes. God made us all in His image, and there are no wimps among His children. However, you will not unlock His glory within you until you do what He commands.

3. God abhors cowards, rejects them and there will be no cowards in heaven. This explains why we have to shake cowardice off and do whatever God is asking us to do. God was unable to use the fearful soldiers of Gideon's army because those who are ruled by fear can never accomplish divine tasks (Judges 7:3,7).

4. No coward can live an obedient life, because obedience and righteousness often demand faith. Such cowards can, therefore, have no testimonies. Cowards didn't openly follow Jesus for fear of being removed from the synagogue (John 12:42-43; 19:38).

ACTION PLAN

Four classic "cardinal" virtues that ought to be woven deeply into the believer's life include wisdom, courage, temperance, and justice respectively. Courage is the virtue that activates every other virtue, and thereby moving us from the category of "good intention" to the far more impressive category of a life well-lived. We are encouraged by Bible stories in our minds, but such courage needs to be tested.

As we daily practice our faith, publicly and in our decision-making and following through, our courage grows. Every step or act of courage makes the next easier for us. It becomes easier to speak against evil, walk in love, resist temptation, and do greater exploits. Courage consequently becomes a habit in our soul.

Jesus Christ's example is courage lived in obedience

to God's holy demand, and for the ultimate welfare of lost sinners and our salvation. I challenge you to move to the next level of courageous exploits today!

CHAPTER 2

SOW THE WORD, REAP WONDERS

The soul can do without everything except the word of God, without which none at all of its wants are provided for. —Martin Luther

The renowned British Evangelist, Rodney "Gipsy" Smith, once recalled an encounter he had with a man who told him that he had never received inspiration from the Bible although he had "gone through it several times." Smith's reply to him was: "Let it go through you once, then you will tell a different story!"

Our attitude to God's word - and not just our access to it - is the most important determinant of our altitude in life. In Mark 4, Jesus gives the parable of the sower thus: "Listen! Behold, a sower went out to sow. And it happened, as he sowed, that some seed fell by the wayside; and the birds of the air came and devoured it. Some fell on stony ground, where it did not have much earth; and immediately it sprang up because it had no depth of earth. But when the sun was up it was scorched, and because it had no root it withered away. And some seed fell among thorns; and the thorns grew up and choked it, and it yielded no crop. But other seed fell on good ground and yielded a crop that sprang up, increased and produced: some thirtyfold, some sixty, and some a hundred."

While explaining the meaning of the parable, Jesus made some critical revelations, from which we must learn vital lessons. To begin with, in verse 11, He says "To you it has been given to know the mystery of the kingdom of God; but to those who are outside, all things come in parables." What this means is that the Kingdom secrets in God's word belong exclusively to Kingdom children. This is why no well-informed believer will utter or agree to a statement like "You never can tell what God will do".

As believers, we can and should know the will of God. 1 John 5:14-15 says, "Now this is the confidence that we have in Him, that if we ask anything according to His will, He hears us. And if we know that He hears us, whatever we ask, we know that we have the petitions that we have asked of Him." The most fulfilling aspect of prayer is the confidence that God hears us because we are within the sphere of His will at all times. To have this assurance is to have what we have asked Him for. If we don't know the will of God, let's dig into His word and stop making excuses.

Jesus made a distinction between His audiences - the "you" (the insiders) to whom revelation has been given by God; and the outsiders who only hear parables. Insiders are believers who have learned the "mystery" referred to as "the truth" that is hidden and can only be known if God reveals it (Daniel 2:18-19, 27-30, 47). It does not refer to esoteric knowledge or secret rites that are discoverable by human effort.

DISSECTING THE PARABLE

The Scripture tells us that the sower sows the seed – which is the word of God; and it is the incorruptible seed which never fails to produce. If you are not getting desired results as anticipated in any area of life, it could be that you are not planting the incorruptible seed, since there can be no germination or harvest if there is no seed.

The reason for many unanswered prayers is the failure to grasp this principle of corresponding action. It is, of course, vital to really understand the principle of seed-time-harvest. Before you can say, "here it is" (harvest), you certainly must have planted and allowed a waiting time to tarry. This is an essential pre-requisite and a process you cannot circumvent.

Moreover, it is critical that we recognize that the soil is our "heart", and if we keep digging up what we have planted, through ungodly attitudes such as unbelief, doubt and complaining, we will destroy our harvest. Satan recognizes that the word of God is settled and incorruptible, and thus cannot stop it. What he does instead is to devise strategies to prevent the word from taking root in our lives.

GETTING THE BEST FROM THE WORD

Despite the tricks of the devil, you can make God's word continually work for you by observing the following:

1. Get clear revelation from the word: Satan often steals the word and prevents it from bearing fruit in people's lives when blind religious devotion, meaningless traditions, wrong doctrines or evil communication is allowed to becloud the mind from receiving the interpretation and inspiration of the Spirit of God. 1 Corinthians 15:33-34 says, "Do not be deceived: "Evil company corrupts good habits." Awake to righteousness, and do not sin..."

Jesus, in His interpretation of the wayside seeds says, "And these are the ones by the wayside where the word is sown. When they hear, Satan comes immediately and takes away the word that was sown in their hearts" (verse 11). Matthew 13:19 puts it this way, "When anyone hears the word of the kingdom, and does not understand it, then the wicked one comes and snatches away what was sown in his heart. This is he who received seed by the wayside."

We must therefore make sure we read or listen attentively to God's word. We must be focused and avoid both physical and psychological distractions because one of Satan's tricks is to ensure that the word is not grasped in our hearts. Satan is not really after you, but you become his enemy the moment you choose to pursue the word because the word overcame him, and he has no antidote for it.

Satan will surely fight and resist you vigorously when you start confessing healing or making prosperity declarations in alignment with God's promises. It is your duty therefore to resolve not to relent in declaring and applying the word. You cannot expect the word to work just by waving the Bible or keeping it idle on your shelf. Sow it into the fertile soil of your heart, through serious study and mediation. The amazing fact is - it is the word that works, not your personal fitness, perfection or holiness.

2. Make the word personal: The second group of people in the parable comprises those likened to the seed that fell on stony ground. Matthew 13:20-21 says, "But he who received the seed on stony places, this is he who hears the word and immediately receives it with joy; yet he has no root in himself, but endures only for a while. For when tribulation or persecution arises because of the word, immediately he stumbles." Those in this category are those who receive the word from others (preachers, pastors, prophets and so on) and were immediately thrilled and apparently lifted in spirit. However, as soon as they face persecution or some other challenges, their faith and enthusiasm crumble.

This is why you need the root of the word in yourself as a believer. You cannot afford to run around on the visions, revelations and prophecies of others. You have to grow and stop being babysat and fed with the teaching of the word. As you take time to develop yourself in the word this way, it becomes easier for you to recall, declare and deploy the word in difficult times, rather than giving in to discouragement and compromise in times of trials and tribulations.

2 Corinthians 10:5 states, "Casting down arguments and every high thing that exalts itself against the knowledge of God, bringing every thought into captivity to the obedience of Christ". Your duty as a believer is to set your mind on the word in the face of resistance, opposition and persecution. John 6:66-

68 says, "From that time many of His disciples went back and walked with Him no more. Then Jesus said to the twelve, "Do you also want to go away?" But Simon Peter answered Him, "Lord to whom we shall go? You have the words of eternal life." Harvests are the results of hard work, not accident.

3. Declutter and shun unwholesome desires: The third soil in the parable represents people who receive the seed of the word among thorns. Thorns here refer to the cares of life, the deceitfulness of riches, worldliness, lusts, and so on – all of which constitute weeds. Since weeds will choke the best seeds, you must declutter, and get rid of unwholesome appetites, lusts, addictions and the likes. According to Matthew 13:22, "Now he who received seed among the thorns is he who hears the word, and the cares of this world and the deceitfulness of riches choke the word, and he becomes unfruitful."

God is never our problem - even while demonstrating His Sovereignty. It is our responsibility to plant the seeds properly, remove the weeds, water the plant, trim out the tares, and remove pests (doubts, unbelief, unforgiveness, and bitterness). In doing this, you conquer all courage-killers and take drastic steps of faith.

4. Courage and fruitfulness are not accidental: The fourth soil, which is the GOOD GROUND, is the one that produces abundant harvests in several folds. As Matthew 13:23 reveals, "But he who received seed on the good ground is he who hears the word and understands it, who indeed bears fruit and produces: some a hundredfold, some sixty, some thirty."

People in this category are those with firm scriptural convictions, which include not associating with, emulating or admiring the ungodly. Psalm 1:1-3 says, "Blessed is the man who walks not in the counsel of the ungodly, nor stands in the path of sinners, nor sits in the seat of the scornful; But his delight is in the law of the Lord, and in His law he meditates day and night. He shall be like a tree planted by the rivers of water, that brings forth its fruit in its season, whose leaf also shall not wither; and whatever he does shall prosper."

Essentially, the scope of impact that the word will have on the soil of your heart and your life in general will depend on how well you have soaked yourself in the word through meditation. Isaiah 28:10 says, "For precept must be upon precept, precept upon precept, line upon line, line upon line, here a little, there a little."

It is of vital importance that the word must always be worked correctly as it demands soaking ourselves in it, rather than dealing with it superficially or rushing through it. We need to soak ourselves in the word to enable us bear root while recognizing that meditation is our key to getting roots beneath and bearing fruits above. Jesus, in John 15:7-8, says, "If you abide in Me, and My words abide in you, you will ask what you desire, and it shall be done for you. By this My Father is glorified, that you bear much fruit; so you will be My disciples." We should use the word appropriately to our advantage as the word is always true.

Ultimately, the four types of soil in the parable of the sower represent types of people and their differing responses to Jesus. The first three types represent those who reject Jesus outright (Matthew 7:26-27) and those who falsely claim to be His disciples (Matthew 7:15-23; 10:35-39). Since bearing the fruits of good deeds is an essential expression of discipleship (Matthew 3:8,10; 7:16-20; 12:33; 21:18-19, 33-34), only those who belong to the last category of recipients of the seed of the word are the true disciples.

Moreover, a harvest of ten to twenty times what was sown is considered a bumper harvest, especially given the primitive agricultural technology of the period. True disciples bear fruit in miraculous numbers.

GOD'S WORD AS YOUR ULTIMATE GUIDE

The following are the reasons why God's word is the ultimate guide to recognize and distinguish His voice, amidst the barrage of voices that we hear from time to time.

1. The word brings peace to the spirit when aligned with His voice. Colossians 3:15-16 states, "And let the peace of God rule in your hearts, to which also you were called in one body; and be thankful. Let the word of Christ dwell in you richly in all wisdom, teaching and admonishing one another in psalms and hymns and spiritual songs, singing with grace in your hearts to the Lord."

Peace is a fruit of the Spirit and it is constant. The peace brought by Christ should always control the believer's heart (Romans 8:16; 15:13; 2 Corinthians 13:11; Galatians 5:22; Ephesians 2:14; Philippians 4:7; 2 Thessalonians 3:16). If you obey the voice of God, your spirit must always have peace about what God wants you to do. Any feeling of agitation or reservation about your decision is not from God. You may need to spend more time in the presence of God, while getting a conflict resolved, as you delight in the Lord and follow the peace in your heart.

2. God has magnified His word above even His name. Philippians 2:9-11 says, "Therefore God also has highly exalted Him and given Him the name which is above every name, that at the name of Jesus every knee should bow, of those in heaven, and of those on earth, and of those under the earth, and that every tongue should confess that Jesus Christ is Lord, to the glory of God the Father."

As the above passage reveals, God gave Jesus a new position, a name that is above every other name. "Every" here includes spatial dimensions - heavens, earth, and under the earth. This is all to the glory of God, while Jesus mediates between God and humans. He is the focus of worship (Lord) and administrator of God's will on earth.

Furthermore, Psalm 138:2 says, "I will worship toward Your holy temple, and praise Your name for Your lovingkindness and Your truth; For You have magnified Your word above all Your name." The fulfillment of God's promises surpasses all previous revelations. High as the name of the Lord is, God has magnified His word above His name.

3. The word is the key to discernment. Every contradiction to the word of God helps us, and facilitates the ability to discern, that the message or suggestion is not from Him. This includes perceptions in our thoughts, intuitions, meditations, and so forth. 1 Thessalonians 5:21-22 says, "Test all things; hold fast what is good. Abstain from every form of evil." Part of what we are to test is the content of prophecies. Everything has to be evaluated with God's truth, as expressed by the Old Testament, Jesus, and the apostles (1 John 4:1-3).

4. God will never violate His word. God never contradicts His word, and anything that contradicts the word of God is certainly not from Him. Numbers 23:19 reveals, "God is not a man, that He should lie, nor a son of man, that He should repent. Has He said, and will He not do? Or has He spoken, and will He not make it good?" Unlike the gods of Mesopotamia, who were often depicted as being whimsical and easily manipulated through sorcery and divination, Balaam could not change what the God of Israel had instructed him to proclaim – blessing for Israel, God's chosen people. Indeed, as Christ says in Matthew 24:35, "Heaven and earth will pass away, but My words will by no means pass away." Jesus' words have the same reliability and enduring quality as every other part of the Scripture.

God's word will never pass away. If anything is to violate the word, it is not coming from Him, it is from the devil. Isaiah 40:8 says, "The grass withers, the flower fades, but the word of our God stands forever."

Humanity is compared to grass and wild flowers, both of which have short-lived and fragile beauty. The contrast is the word of God that endures. Perhaps the contrast also implies that the Babylonians, though seemingly powerful, would fade, but God's word that had promised His people restoration would not fail. Psalms 119:89 adds: "Forever, O Lord, Your word is settled in heaven." The word of God is the central theme of the universe, while the Lord's judgements that maintain order in the cosmos provides for human life as well.

5. God's word prevents from stumbling. The believer must constantly regulate his thoughts, words and actions in line with God's word to avoid being misguided. The psalmist, in Psalms 119:105, states, "Your word is a lamp to my feet and a light to my path."

The lighted path is not whatever we want it to be, but righteous judgments and God's precepts. On such a path, there is no snare but a heritage and rejoicing. Thus, the guidance of the Lord's instructions enables the believer to negotiate right and wrong (Psalms 19:11-13; Proverbs 6:23; John 8:16).

6. The Spirit and the word are one and always agree. 1 John 5:7 says, "For there are three that bear witness in heaven: the Father, the Word, and the Holy

Spirit; and these three are one." This unified witness of the Trinity is supported by other scriptures (See John 10:30; and Amos 3:3 for instance). What God says through His Spirit in us always agrees with what He has said in His word.

7. God's word suffices in all situations. What the believer needs is the wisdom to correctly apply the word to every aspect of our lives since God never speaks out of His word. 2 Timothy 3:16-17 says, "All Scripture is given by inspiration of God, and is profitable for doctrine, for reproof, for correction, for instruction in righteousness, that the man of God may be complete, thoroughly equipped for every good work."

The use of "inspiration" here means that the Scripture was "breathed out" by the Spirit of God. Because the Scripture is from God Himself, it is profitable in many ways, ultimately leading us to righteousness, maturity, and service. "All scripture" refers to the Old Testament, but by implication, to the writings of the New Testament, as well (1 Timothy 5:18; 2 Peter 3:15-16). These verses flow naturally out of 2 Timothy 3:10-17, while the strong statements about the saving and edifying power of the Scripture lead to the command to preach the word (2 Timothy 4:1-4).

Many Christians would have averted colossal marital,

financial, and career failures if they had taken time to study and dig deeper into the Scripture, meditate on it and subsequently hear the voice of God. Jesus Christ even says in John 8:28: "When you lift up the Son of Man, then you will know that I am He, that I do nothing of Myself; but as My Father taught me, I speak these things."

A good knowledge of Christ, as well as hearing from Him, helps us so much to avert embarrassment and disappointments. This is why the WORD must be highly prioritized in our lives at all times.

CHAPTER 3
PERSEVERE TO PREVAIL

Our motto must continue to be perseverance. And ultimately I trust the Almighty will crown our efforts with success. —William Wilberforce

I must first and foremost thank God Almighty and give Him the glory for keeping me alive to be able to relate how I survived a remarkable ordeal in the forested jungle of Southern Oregon in the Northwest fringe of the US. The incident occurred in 1974, just as I was about to graduate with a Bachelor of Science (BS) in Geology from the University of Oregon, Eugene. It was to be the climax of the lifelong dream I had conceived since 1962, after graduating from high school in Ogbomoso, Nigeria.

After overcoming various unbelievable hurdles and challenges, I had travelled for the first time out of Nigeria to begin my university education in 1970 in U.S.A. By 1974, I had just a major and only one requirement left in my degree course work - a field mapping practical project - to finally obtain my qualification. However, I had in the previous year been diagnosed with rheumatoid arthritis which had invaded all my bone joints and caused severe pains all over my body. The rheumatologist physician had prescribed a daily maximum dosage of aspirin to barely relieve me of severe pains.

Unfortunately, the University of Oregon maintained a very strict pre-requisite and ultimate requirement for getting a Geology degree. I appealed and passionately requested for a waiver, based on medical grounds, to skip the mapping project requirements. Despite all the sound medical rationale to secure a waiver for me to undertake a substitute assignment, the university administration declined me and advised that I considered switching my major degree from Geology. This was a particularly difficult decision-making period, but I stood my ground on getting a Geology degree.

With the advantage of hindsight, I can say that it was really a "Goliath" the "David" in me had to contend with. All I remember today is that I had that unquenchable fire inside me to obtain a Geology degree and eventually serve in the oil and gas industry. Since the university administrators declined to give me a waiver, I inevitably had to undertake the mapping project.

PRESSED BEYOND MEASURE

We had to camp for the entire three months duration of the project on Mount Ashland, at about 8,000 feet above sea-level, which caused cold weather, despite being the summer season since it was a relatively high altitude. This posed another major health challenge for me.

The camp project itself involved three major mapping projects, to be conducted individually, based on geologic mapping concepts. We had to carry out the mapping exercise during the daytime in groups of two (paired into individual mapping blocks) to monitor each other's tracking safety. We planned to return to the base camp in time before it got dark every day.

After a couple of weeks working on this daily mapping exercise, it became extremely challenging on my physical fitness, due to arthritic pains constantly inflicted on my joints and bones. This, notwithstanding, I was focused while fixing my mind always on the end product of anticipated accomplishment – a bachelor's degree in Geology. This virtually kept me going, despite very severe pains. It was a period I can well refer to as the "torture" episode of my life.

The cold spells on the mountain aggravated pains in my body. There were days in the camp I very strongly felt like quitting and returning home to the registrar's office to change my major course. However, I could not just accept quitting Geology, when I was so close to the very end of the entire program! (After three years on the degree program).

STRANDED BUT SAFEGUARDED

The cumbersome episode peaked on the day I suddenly could not navigate my way back to the camp in daytime after the day's mapping exercise. Apparently, I got incredibly fatigued with pains all over my legs and joints, and was not fast enough on my way back to the field camp. It became dark and I was forced to spend the night staying on a small clearing within the very tall wooded forest. I noticed that small helicopters later paraded the location where I got stranded for quite for some time, but they apparently quitted on me since it was dark and I was invisible, far below the tall timbers in the jungle of Mount Ashland in Southern Oregon/California border.

I recall that, being tired, I dozed off a number of times, but did not sleep at all, as it was pitch dark! And we had been earlier briefed before the trip that the forest was a habitat for polar bears. I remember pacing the small bush clearing to keep me alert and awake.

Two other events I consider as my life's major survival miracles happened on this same night. First, the night duration spent, as it seemed to me, was incredibly short! Second, it took me just about twenty minutes to navigate back to the field camp, as soon as there was enough daylight for me to view the compass being used for navigation. I miraculously just walked straight back to the field camp, Hallelujah!! The Lord is indeed my shepherd! (Psalm 23:1)

The rest is history! I eventually obtained a graduate degree in Geology (in 1977), became a professional in the oil and gas industry, and currently a geology professor in the university. Perseverance has ultimately paid off!

BECOMING PERSEVERANT

Perseverance is the steadfast pursuit of a goal, in spite of difficulty, opposition, or even failures. The good news is that it is a Christian virtue, as God doesn't want us to be quitters. Luke 9:62 says, "But Jesus said to him, "No one, having put his hand to the plow, and looking back, is fit for the kingdom of God."

Christians, for example, cannot follow Christ by looking back. We must focus on serving Him as we move ahead at His command. Apostle Paul shows us his own example in Philippians 3:13-14, saying: "Brethren,

I do not count myself to have apprehended; but one thing I do, forgetting those things which are behind and reaching forward to those things which are ahead, I press toward the goal for the prize of the upward call of God in Christ Jesus."

Paul used the athletics' imagery of a runner's energy and focus, as well as his eventual reward, when he is called upon to the platform to receive the winning prize. Other scriptures on the virtue of perseverance and the desire of God for us not to be quitters include Proverbs 24:16 and Galatians 6:9.

To prevail in life through perseverance, you need to be mindful of the following truths:

- God hates quitters.
- Quitters quit because their faith fails.
- You might just quit before your breakthrough.
- Quitters are losers; they never win anything.
- Our foremost reward for persevering is that we reach our goal.
- Perseverance helps to bring answer to our prayers and fulfillment of our expected miracles.

KEY AREAS OF PERSEVERANCE

In actual fact, perseverance is a key virtue that must be rooted in our nature and must reflect in every area of our lives. However, the following specific areas are of utmost significance:

1. Our Christian journey. The Christian race is full of battles, challenges, trials, temptations and persecutions that can easily discourage and derail us, if we cannot persevere. That aside, the very nature of the Christian life, which involves doing good and spreading the light of the gospel, cannot be accomplished without a daily attitude of perseverance. Galatians 6:8-10 says, "For he who sows to his flesh will of the flesh reap corruption, but he who sows to the Spirit will of the Spirit reap everlasting life. And let us not grow weary while doing good, for in due season we shall reap if we do not lose heart."

Our Christian journey involves a number of vital areas of attention and a mixed grill such as fervent prayer, fellowship, Bible study, evangelism, constant communion with God, and so on. Indeed, it is a marathon race, which means that we must not grow weary or lose heart if we must win. Regarding the above admonition in Galatians, doing good is not seeking to be justified by works, but living as God has planned for those who have received His gracious salvation through faith (Ephesians 2:8-10). To "sow to the spirit" over the long haul means taking the opportunity that the Lord has placed before us to work for the good of all.

2. Raising godly homes and families. Husbands are exhorted to love their wives, while wives are admonished to submit to their husbands (Ephesians 5:22-28). Children are enjoined to honor their parents, while the parents (fathers in particular) are instructed not to provoke their children but raise them in the nurture and admonition of the Lord (Ephesians 6:1-4). All these require a great deal of perseverance because of human shortcomings and frailties.

Apostle Peter also gives a word of wisdom on how wives and husbands should conduct themselves in the family. 1 Peter 3:5-7 states, "For in this manner, in former times, the holy women who trusted in God also adorned themselves, being submissive to their own husbands, as Sarah obeyed Abraham, calling him lord, whose daughters you are if you do good and are not afraid with any terror. Husbands, likewise, dwell with them with understanding, giving honor to the wife, as to the weaker vessel, and as being heirs together of the grace of life, that your prayers may not be hindered."

Peter commanded husbands to live in harmony with their wives and to treat them as fellow inheritors of salvation and its privileges. "Weaker" refers to physical strength, and not to be taken to mean that wives are morally or intellectually inferior to their husbands.

3. Giving. We cannot be tired of giving as believers, especially when we know that our harvests are in our seeds! Luke 6:38 says, "Give, and it will be given to you: good measure, pressed down, shaken together, and running over will be put into your bosom. For with the same measure that you use, it will be measured back to you."

"Measure" involves weighing and judging, and it is vital to be fair to others in the process, since the same measure you use will eventually return to you. If you are generous, generosity will be returned to you in full measure. If you are stingy and uncharitable, such will be the standards by which you are judged.

2 Corinthians 9:6-9 also says, "But this I say: He who sows sparingly will also reap sparingly, and he who sows bountifully will also reap bountifully. So let each one give as he purposes in his heart, not grudgingly or of necessity; for God loves a cheerful giver. And God is able to make all grace abound toward you, that you, always having all sufficiency in all things, may have an abundance for every good work. As it is written: "He has dispersed abroad, He has given to the poor; His righteousness endures forever."

God in His Sovereignty loves a cheerful giver. He allows each person to give as he purposes in his heart in a way that will make him be at peace with himself based on individual decisions. The words "sparingly" and "bountifully" outline a principle that is proverbially true, based on common agricultural context, as well as its application in financial matters. "All grace", "all sufficiency", "all things", and "every good work", are closely related expressions and are repeatedly used to extol God's blessings.

4. Receiving some miracles and breakthroughs. Not all prayers receive instant answers. Hebrews 10:35-36 says, "Therefore do not cast away your confidence, which has great reward. For you have need of endurance, so that after you have done the will of God, you may receive the promise." The believer must understand the hidden fact that between when you say "Amen" and "there it is", you need faith not to abort your miracle by quitting. Hebrews 11:6 admonishes, "But without faith it is impossible to please Him, for he who comes to God must believe that He is, and that He is a rewarder of those who diligently seek Him."

Also, in Mark 11:22-24, Jesus says, "Have faith in God. For assuredly, I say to you, whoever says to this mountain, 'Be removed and be cast into the sea,' and does not doubt in his heart, but believes that those things he says will be done, he will have whatever he says. Therefore I say to you, whatever things you ask when you pray, believe that you receive them, and you will have them."

MODELS OF PERSEVERANCE

1. The woman with the issue of blood suffered a spiteful disease for 12 years and was ripped off by charlatans, who promised healing but gave nothing. She bluntly refused to give up till she got healed by faith through touching of the helm of Jesus' gown (Luke 8:43-48).

2. Hannah, in spite of torments and insults year after year (while her husband's junior wife teased her on being childless; and being thought to be in a drunken spell because she prayed to God passionately with mumbling in the temple), persevered till she had her son (1 Samuel 1:6; 14-20).

3. The paralyzed man, as well as his four friends, who carried and dropped him from the roof of a crowded hall, in order to be healed by Jesus (Mark 2:1-5).

4. The persistent widow that would not relent but kept pestering the wicked judge until he succumbed to avenge for her (Luke 18:1-5).

5. Job, who endured a lengthy period of affliction, despite being righteous, but was eventually vindicated. The Scripture asks us to emulate him: "Indeed we count them blessed who endure. You have heard of the perseverance of Job and seen the end intended by the Lord—that the Lord is very compassionate and merciful" (James 5:11).

WILL YOU PASS THE TEST?

God has not made us to be wimps; therefore, we must persevere through life's journey, since perseverance is a necessary Christian virtue for our purpose on earth to be accomplished. We must ever be conscious that the longer things get, the closer we are to reaching our goals.

As a believer, you must refuse to look back. Don't give up on your dreams and your endeavors despite the challenges that may come your way. Quitters often end up as failures - and this is never God's purpose for your life as his ambassador on earth. Whenever you are tempted to ask that "this cup" be taken from you, don't forget to add in holy submission, "nevertheless, not my will but Yours be done" (Luke 22:42). This was the ultimate example Christ laid for us, as He faced sacrificial death with an obedient courage in response to God's purpose for our salvation.

Remember always that only those who stand firm - that is, persevere to the end - will be saved.

CHAPTER 4

MASTER YOUR MIND

You have power over your mind, not outside events. Realize this, and you will find strength. —Marcus Aurelius

One fundamental truth you must recognize is that you are not in any way ordinary. You are a spirit-being, who possesses a soul (mind) and lives in a physical body (the flesh). The spirit is the real believer, while the mind is the powerhouse of emotions, intellect, imaginations, will, attitudes, memory, reasoning, and perceptions.

The mind is "programmed" and often influenced by past experiences, as well as beliefs and assumptions acquired from culture, tradition, shared knowledge and the likes. If all these factors are not consciously interrogated, methodically mastered and properly aligned, they could trigger a shipwrecked life.

You are ultimately what you think you are. Your thoughts significantly influence your ability to achieve tangible and buoyant results in life. Proverbs 23:7a says, "But as he thinks in his heart, so is he…" Eventually, the inner character of a person will show and be displayed outside.

Genesis 11:6 also reveals, "And the Lord said, "Indeed the people are one and they all have one language, and this is what they begin to do; now nothing that they propose to do will be withheld from them." God's concern that nothing the people might purpose to do would be withheld from them does not express a divine a fear that humans might someday become as powerful as God. It rather conveys dismay that people, unchecked, would undertake extraordinary deeds of evil and defiance that could emanate from inner-man potential.

Believers often fall short of God's best purposes for their lives because they allow their minds to rob them of what He already prepared for them. Classic examples in scriptures include the Israelites, who failed to enter the promised land; and Peter, who sank while walking on water as soon as he looked away from Jesus (Numbers 13; Matthew 14:22-31). Despite that God's plans and promises were very clear in both cases, doubt and fear hindered the people from attaining God's best. Incidentally, the same is true about believers today, but we can decide right now not to allow these "mind sicknesses" to limit us any longer.

HOW TO MASTER YOUR MIND

1. Feed your mind with a healthy diet: A believer's strong spirit can withstand any storm of life, and it is required to stabilize the wavering tendencies of the mind. Proverbs 18:14 says, "The spirit of a man will sustain him in sickness, but who can bear a broken spirit?" Proverbs. 24:10 adds, "If you faint in the day of adversity, Your strength is small."

To faint is to go slack, and adversity is literally restriction. You must constantly feed your mind to avoid losing strength. Believers build spiritual strength by praying in the Holy Ghost (Jude 1:20), while this process is maintained by feeding on a "healthy" diet of the word of God which requires meditation (1 Timothy 4:6; Joshua 1:8).

1 Peter 2:2 instructs us to desire the word of God, just like a baby desires milk to grow. We must realize that the goal of meditation is not to fulfill a religious obligation, but rather to acquire nourishment essential for growth Mark 4:24-25 says, "Then He said to them, "Take heed what you hear. With the same measure you use, it will be measured to you; and to you who hear, more will be given. For whoever has, to him more

will be given; but whoever does not have, even what he has will be taken away from him." Hearing is vital (Romans 10:17), and God will grant more revelation and understanding to those who listen and respond; but some others will neither hear nor benefit from revelation – to their own detriment.

2. Guard your mind: Your mind functions and governs your life – according to what you allow into it. This calls for utmost vigilance. Proverbs 4:23 says, "Keep your heart with all diligence, for out of it spring the issues of life." The effective way to guard your mind is to always monitor its entry and exit points of information and ideas. You must watch over and shield it from harmful contents from the environment, physically and spiritually.

To guard and master your mind, you will have to keep an eye on what comes in through your "eye-gate" and your "ear-gate". Regarding the "eye-gate", we have a good illustration in Matthew 14:28-30, "And Peter answered Him and said, "Lord, if it is You, command me to come to You on the water." So He said, "Come." And when Peter had come down out of the boat, he walked on the water to go to Jesus. But when he saw that the wind was boisterous, he was afraid; and beginning to sink he cried out, saying, "Lord, save me!"

Peter gave in to fear and began to sink once he shifted

his focus from Jesus (the Word) to the wind and other physical threats around him. For the "ear-gate", the Scripture records that the hearts of the Israelites also melted, perplexed in fear, after hearing the "evil report" from the ten spies earlier sent to spy the land of the enemy they wanted to fight (See Numbers 14:1).

Knowing all these therefore requires that you take practical steps to guard your eye- and ear-gates. These include: Scrutinizing what you listen to and watch (especially in these days of social media distractions); streamlining your circle of influence. Proverbs 13:20 says, "He who walks with wise men will be wise, but the companion of fools will be destroyed." 1 Corinthians 15:33 states, "Do not be deceived: "Evil company corrupts good habits"; keeping the word in front of your eyes – which could include carrying it on flash cards and pasting scriptures at strategic places in your car and home (Proverbs 4:20-21); as well as developing a habit of actively listening to the word and speaking it in faith (Romans 10:17; Mark 11:23; Joshua 3:4-5).

3. Renew your mind: You have to change the way you think for renewal to be effective on your mind. This implies that you stop the old thought process and start aligning your thoughts with the word of God. Romans 12:1-2 admonishes , "I beseech you therefore, brethren, by the mercies of God, that you present your bodies a living sacrifice, holy, acceptable to God, which is your reasonable service. And do not be conformed to this world, but be transformed by the renewing of your mind, that you may prove what is that good and acceptable and perfect will of God."

This process demands diligence, which requires you to honestly and periodically re-examine yourself by: evaluating your thoughts, passing them through the "litmus test" of thinking, promptly casting out the wrong thoughts, and replacing them with the truth of God's word (2 Corinthians 10:4-5; Ephesians 6:11-17).

Our service entails dedication of the total person to living for God's honor. Christians must be different from non-Christians, and we should experience progressive transformation of life by renewing our mind. The mind is changed by prayer, by reading and reflection on God's word, by worship, and by meditation on God's acts, as the Holy Spirit works in us. Philippians 4:8 says it well, "Finally, brethren, whatever things are true, whatever things are noble, whatever things are just, whatever things are pure, whatever things are lovely, whatever things are of good report, if there is any virtue and if there is anything praiseworthy—meditate on these things."

Seven components of the kinds of thoughts that help to renew our minds are mentioned in the above passage:

- "True" – which means "ethical" or "honest";

- "noble" – which means "respectable" or "honorable";

- "Just" – which is giving people what they deserve;

- "Lovely" means "attractive" (mentioned only here in the New Testament);

- "Pure" means "holy" in relation to God;

- "Of good report" means praiseworthy (also used here in the NT); and

- "Virtue" refers to "moral excellence".

4. Fix your mind in confident expectation: Now that you have sown potent "word-seeds" into your future through your spirit-man (mind), you must be very careful not to allow your mind to wander unguarded, and thereby rob you of your harvest. You have to arrest and anchor your mind, keeping it fixed in "confident expectation" of a good harvest.

CHARACTERISTICS OF GREAT THINKERS

Out of the heart proceed the issues of life – so says the Scripture (Proverbs 4:23). Simply put, our thoughts control our lives and, on a larger scale, ideas rule the world. Most of the progress the world has continued to enjoy has been through the efforts of thinkers who are maximizing their God-given ideas to bless humanity. The most paramount attributes of these great individuals, which we all can emulate, are:

- They think with their hearts
- They are on fire
- They live their lives with a purpose
- They never lose their imagination
- They turn reality into fantasy
- They don't take no for an answer (never quit)
- They marinate their thoughts
- They think better together.

BECOMING A GREAT THINKER

It is a very terrible thing to allow the mind to rot away, being the most powerful machine that God has made and in-built into the human spirit. Henry Ford remarked that thinking is the hardest work to do, which explains why so few persevere to engage in it. Victor Hugo expressed this viewpoint with greater precision when he says, "An invading army can be resisted, but no one can resist the invasion of extraordinary ideas."

Scientific research has revealed that we use only 10% of our brains usually; such that when we are challenged to think outside the box, we are consequently challenged to fantasize and compelled to deploy the remaining 90% of our brain's capacity. Scripture shows us the example of Jacob in Genesis 30. He had literally slaved for 14 years - the first 7 years for Leah and the second for Rachael – and then laboring with no stable income. Jacob was forced to think creatively, out of the box, with the 90% of his unused brain capacity. Then he struck his "REHOBOTH" or "eureka!" – he found a brilliant idea that increased his flocks creatively.

I once read the story of a hairdresser who did the hair of a celebrity in 30 minutes with a mere ribbon. The irony is that it wasn't the ribbon that did the marvelous work - since the ribbon was a free item anyway; it was the creative genius of the hairdresser. You will be exempted from invaluable energy exertion that leads you nowhere once you recognize the value of a powerful idea.

One brilliant idea is purposeful, and is of better value, than a million activities. New ideas and trials should be constantly paraded, as doing the same thing repeatedly and expecting new results is a futile process. Creative thinkers are wildcat explorers, who dare to ask new questions since they know that every problem breeds its own solution. They equally believe that every solution can yet breed a better answer, and taken to another higher level of rationalization.

It is of vital importance to realize that if you capitalize on your idea, you will shift your own worth in a huge way, transform the culture, and make a lasting impact and difference on the human race. Ideas rule the world, and it is paramount to discover the process for developing great ideas.

Some of the creative men in Scriptures include Solomon, who was exceptional (1 Kings 3:12; Proverbs 23:7), Jacob (Genesis 31), Jesus (Luke 19:14-17) and Bezaleel (Exodus 35:30-35). In contemporary times, great thinkers include Martin Luther King Jr., Walt Disney, Steve Job, Ted Turner, and so forth.

PERSONAL DIVIDENDS OF CREATIVITY

Let me share with you how I diversified from an oil industry professional career, after 25 years, and shifted worth to a higher level in academic lectureship to date. It was not an easy journey, but glory to God Almighty for enabling me to transfer to a professional academic career, which involves teaching geology, weather, ocean, and climate studies in the university.

I believe that there is a new, vital, raw, brazen idea

for every one of us that can keep us ahead, help us resolve financial, career and family complications, as well as keep us whole, while we move our world forward. From my past experiences, I have come to realize that there are no limits to those that can think creatively. It is important to be aware of the fact that there are opportunities we can harness to enrich our activities wherever we conduct our duties. It is left for us however, to discover it as believers, based on the spiritual, political, and socio-economic climate of the environment.

As I noted above, after 25 years of professional career in the oil industry, I decided to diversify to the academic profession, being in line with my long term plans. The oil and gas industry had been unstable, with the usual crude oil price in a state of "yoyo", causing the price of oil to reach rock bottom. This culminated in most multinationals' frequent "lay-offs" plus reduction of investment in oil and gas development.

Major multinational oil companies bought over and acquired various other smaller oil operations and service companies (including the company where I worked) which inevitably led to layoffs and job scarcity. Large number of industry professionals invaded the academic institutions for employment. I accepted an instructor position in a junior college for a part time job, since the job market was inundated.

Quite unexpectedly, the situation grew worse and in less than two years, my gloomy financial condition began to adversely affect my personal and family livelihood. I became frustrated after laboring on part-time jobs with no stable incomes, and I realized I had to think creatively, out of the box, with the remaining 90% of my unused brain capacity.

About this time, the faithful God apparently sent to me a "divine connector" to give me a golden advice, which eventually gave me a breakthrough to the current professional academic position in a university. The divine messenger happened to be the chair of the Geology department where I was teaching on a part-time contract basis. Dr. Dwight Kranz said he realized I was underemployed due to the downturn in the job market, and he suggested that I would be guaranteed a "niche" for a stable, fulltime academic instructor's employment, if I trained and acquired the skills required to teach online (online education). He predicted that by the year 2000, online education would be providing academic instructors stable employment to replace the traditional face-to-face classroom instruction method, due to the needs of professional students.

Fortunately, I promptly trained in appropriate computer software, acquired online instructions skills, and started teaching both hybrid and fully online courses within nine months. This period coincided with when higher education institutions (junior colleges and universities) began to hire instructors that had online teaching experience. I became more stabilized on my part-time employment, and more marketable, such that I was hired for a lecturer position at the University of Houston–Downtown. Glory be to the merciful God for sending me a "divine connector" who directed me to my breakthrough through the difficult channel of my career diversification from the industrial sector, after so many years, to a brand new sector in academia.

GREATER HEIGHTS

Further to this major career diversification and development, I intentionally sought for even more opportunities to advance my online instruction skills. Incidentally, I was the only online instructor from 2006 till 2009 at the Natural Science Department, University of Houston-Downtown (UH-D). I tasked my personal expenses to obtain certification to teach college-level applied science courses from the American Meteorological Society (AMS) education curriculum on weather, ocean, and climate studies.

These courses soon began to compete successfully with the existing traditional science courses in our department, and all semesters courses (including mini-mesters, and summer semesters) were always completely filled up by students' enrollment. The Natural Science Department had to advertise specially for additional instructors to meet the rapidly rising students' enrollment. Classes offered in weather, ocean, and climate studies respectively rose from two sections in 2004 to 25 sections currently in 2018.

The point here is that if you dare to aim higher and advance your vision, you will tremendously shift your own worth, transform the culture, and make a lasting impact and difference. Invariably, we are forced to go beyond the regular use of just 10% of our brains, and challenged to think creatively, out of the box, with the unused part of the brain. Hallelujah, we give glory and honor to God Almighty for all these amazing provisions!

CHAPTER 5

EXAMINE YOUR LOYALTY

A wife who is 85% faithful to her husband is not faithful at all. There is no such thing as part-time loyalty to Jesus Christ. —Vance Havner

True loyalty is a state of being constant and faithful, bearing true allegiance. Loyalty manifests in unmistakable and unshakable devotion. It is devoid of pretense, shame, fickleness or double-mindedness. This is what makes it an essential virtue for success in our Christian race and in life in general.

The depth of our loyalty can seen in our commitment to our relationship with God, even in seemingly bad times - as well as in our commitment to those whom God has brought into our lives and has called us to serve, even under the most difficult circumstances. Proverbs 17:17 says, "A friend loves at all times, and a brother is born for adversity." One purpose of a relative is to uphold a family member in adversity (Leviticus 25:25, 47-48). An unlikely but possible interpretation is that a friend is better because he loves at all times, not just in difficult times.

Loyalty is also typified in human relationships and God's covenant relations with His people. Deuteronomy 7:9 states, "Therefore know that the Lord your God, He is God, the faithful God who keeps covenant and mercy for a thousand generations with those who love Him and keep His commandments". "A thousand generation" is a term denoting an immeasurable future and not a specific span of time. God's covenant of mercy is boundless and unending. Though Israel (and mankind in general) might prove to be unfaithful to the Lord, the promises of God to the nation cannot fail to be fulfilled (Deuteronomy 30:1-10; Jer. 31:31-34; Ezekiel 36:24-32; Romans 11:29).

God expects us to be loyal to Him. In 1 Chronicles 29:18, King David states, "O Lord God of Abraham, Isaac, and Israel, our fathers, keep this forever in the intent of the thoughts of the heart of Your people, and fix their heart toward You." As David continued to focus on God, he acknowledged that it is not possible to offer anything to God because He owns everything. David also declared that it is not possible to deceive God since He knows exactly who is giving willingly out of true devotion to Him, and who is giving just to be seen by others. The hallmark of Christian loyalty therefore is a heart that wants to please God at all times.

Moses had a sure testimony of being loyal to God. God, in Numbers 12:7 says of him, "Not so with My servant Moses; He is faithful in all My house." Caleb had a similar testimony (Numbers 14:24). Joshua boldly declared the loyalty of his household to God in Joshua 24:14-15, "Now therefore, fear the Lord, serve Him in sincerity and in truth, and put away the gods which your fathers served on the other side of the River and in Egypt. Serve the Lord! And if it seems evil to you to serve the Lord, choose for yourselves this day whom you will serve, whether the gods which your fathers served that were on the other side of the River, or the gods of the Amorites, in whose land you dwell. But as for me and my house, we will serve the Lord."

God's demand stipulated that the people of Israel (and indeed the whole earth) serve Him only. The pertinent fact here is, we all have our loyalties, but the real question is, to what or to whom are we loyal? Let's take a deeper look at dimensions of loyalty.

LOYALTY TO GOD

The Bible instructs us to love the Lord with all our hearts, with all our soul and with all our strength

(Deuteronomy 6:5). Parents must teach God's instructions to their children with strong intentionality that manifests in diligent instruction by word and deed. The kind of love that God requires is one that is full time and under every circumstance. Children must therefore be taught to love Him in the same way. Matthew 22:37-38 reiterates this, "Jesus said to him, "You shall love the Lord your God with all your heart, with all your soul, and with all your mind.' This is the first and great commandment."

The best time to assess the depth of our loyalty is when we face challenging situations. This is akin to squeezing juice out of an orange. You will only get to know how much juice the orange has when you have squeezed it to the breaking point. To explain this better, the following are a few Bible characters who were squeezed to such a breaking point to reveal their loyalty or otherwise:

1. Daniel. He remained loyal, even when squeezed hard to face the king's wrath. He chose to defy the decree of the king by openly praying toward Jerusalem, for which reason he was thrown into the lion's den – Daniel 6:10.

2. Peter. He swore his loyalty to Jesus 100%, but when it became obvious that he might share in the Savior's rejection and death, he denied Him three times – Matthew 26:35, 75.

3. Saul. He was very loyal to the Jewish religion and faithfully persecuted the early Christians until he encountered Jesus on the way to Damascus. He afterwards, as Paul, proved to have unwavering loyalty to Jesus, for which Nero sentenced him to death – Acts 9:3-6; 2 Timothy 4:6-7.

4. The three Hebrew men, Shadrach, Meshach and Abednego boldly defied King Nebuchadnezzar's decree that everyone who heard the sound of musical instruments with all kinds of music should fall down and worship the golden image. They refused to bow, in loyalty to the God of Israel. They were cast into a burning fiery furnace, with the heat seven times more than it was usually heated – (Daniel 3). Their faith in God did not rest on the belief that He would perform a miracle, but that their sovereign God could be trusted. They asserted that if God chose not to deliver them from the king's punishment but instead allowed them to become martyrs for Him, they would still refuse to serve the king's gods or the image. This is one of the strongest demonstrations of steadfast faith and loyalty in the Bible.

LOYALTY TO THE FAMILY

God expects believers to have an unwavering loyalty to our families, especially to our marriages. Genesis 2:24 commands, "Therefore a man shall leave his father and mother and be joined to his wife, and they shall become one flesh." God's timeless design for marriage, declared as a one-flesh relationship, certainly involves sexual union; but it also includes a husband and wife coming together in spiritual, mental, and emotional harmony.

God ordained marriage by creation and by command. He created two complementary genders, male and female, and commanded one man and one woman to unite in marriage. Therefore, human efforts to dissolve marriage constitute an attack on God's own work, since He ordained it.

The marriage commitment takes precedence over every other human relationship. "One flesh" means closely joined, and it hallows the biblical standard of covenantal heterosexual marital relationship, while excluding polygamy and adultery. Essentially, marriage is primarily a divine ordinance, graciously and lovingly designed for mutual satisfaction and delight.

God hates divorce. He wants us to remain ever loyal to our mate. Malachi 2:16 says, "For the Lord God of Israel says that He hates divorce, for it covers one's garment with violence…" All marital vows are usually publicly declared. Apart from the bride and bridegroom, God and wedding attendees witness marital vows (Malachi 2:14).

An exceptional biblical and classic example of an unwavering loyalty to marital vows was demonstrated by Ruth in refusing to turn away even after the death of her husband. She remained loyal to his family. Ruth 1:15-17 states, "And she said, "Look, your sister-in-law has gone back to her people and to her gods; return after your sister-in-law." But Ruth said: "Entreat me not to leave you, Or to turn back from following after you; For wherever you go, I will go; And wherever you lodge, I will lodge; Your people shall be my people, and your God, my God. Where you die, I will die, and there will I be buried. The Lord do so to me, and more also, if anything but death parts you and me." Ruth was not moved by the intensity of Naomi's attempts to dissuade her from accompanying her back to Bethlehem. She bound herself to go with Naomi and to lodge with her, and would even die and be buried where Naomi was – the greatest possible commitment in the ancient world.

Other forms of family loyalty are expressed in the Scripture. In marriage, a lady's allegiance shifts from her parents to her husband (Numbers 30:5-8). God instructs on honoring our father and mother. He says in Exodus 20:12: " Honor your father and your mother, that your days may be long upon the land which the Lord your God is giving you." Eli's sons showed contempt for their father and for the Lord, which resulted in their untimely death (1 Samuel 2:12-17, 22-25, 29-30).

The respect and kindness that Jacob and Ruth showed to their respective parents provide positive examples (Proverbs 1:8; 19:26; 20:20; 23:22; 28:24, 30:17). Failure to honor parents was one of the sins that Ezekiel and Micah listed in a description of the people of Jerusalem before the city was destroyed (Ezekiel 22:7; Micah 7:6). Long life for individuals can be an outcome from the Lord for loyal obedience (Exodus 23:26).

LOYALTY TO AUTHORITY

The Bible reveals that the powers that exist are ordained by God. Romans 13:1-3 says, "Let every soul be subject to the governing authorities. For there is no authority except from God, and the authorities that exist are appointed by God. Therefore whoever resists the authority resists the ordinance of God, and those who resist will bring judgment on themselves. For rulers are not a terror to good works, but to evil. Do you want to be unafraid of the authority? Do what is good, and you will have praise from the same." God is sovereign over human affairs, and unwarranted rebellion against government is rebellion against God. Government is ordained by God to reward good and punish evil, providing peace and order for those whom it serves. The Jewish nation rebelled against Rome in two costly wars, bringing judgement upon themselves at a cost of more than one million lives. A government that rewards evil and punishes good will not long survive, for evil is innately destructive. He who is perverse in his way will suddenly fall, says Proverbs 28:18.

It is of vital civil and spiritual importance to re-examine the process of improving on your loyalty to authority. You need to think and refine the steps you will adopt to always obey civil authorities such as your employers, church leaders, police, your boss at work, and even community leaders. You need to always reverence and respect all these authorities.

Of course, there might be occasions when certain authorities to whom you are loyal might disappoint you. The ultimate solution to such a situation is that your focus should always be on God's word, rather than on people.

MAKING YOUR LOYALTY COUNT

To sum up our discussion on loyalty, take note of the following again:

1. Loyalty to God is always rewarding and ultimate.

2. Loyalty is what you do, not what you say. Talk

is cheap, while loyalty is seen in your action, particularly in difficult times.

3. Loyalty can be demanding and sacrificial, demanding that you prove your loyalty at premium costs - sometimes to do something huge or demanding.

4. Loyalty does not waver. It involves the steady involvement and commitment to our relationship responsibilities in God and His kingdom.

5. Loyalty is willful resolve. When you force it, it is not real. You have to make up your mind to align with God on matters of loyalty, unlike the rich young ruler in Mark 10:17-22 who was not loyal.

6. Divided loyalty is no loyalty – 2 Kings 17:33; Matthew 6:24.

7. God frowns on disloyalty. Nothing short of wholehearted service to the Lord will suffice – Hosea 6:4-5; Psalm 78:8; 37.

CHAPTER 6
YOUR REFUGE IN A RESTLESS WORLD

The secret of his presence is a more secure refuge than a thousand Gibraltars. I do not mean that no trials come. They may come in abundance, but they cannot penetrate into the sanctuary of the soul, and we may dwell in perfect peace even in the midst of life fiercest storms. —Hannah Whitall Smith

A general overview of current world affairs reveals an alarming display of unethical practices in governance. It has become more difficult to trust most leaders because of fraudulent practices, financial embezzlement political gimmicks and pathological lying. We frequently hear rumors of impending wars, nuclear weapon proliferations, and international power play politics.

International allies and security unions across the world often break their treaties suddenly with impunity.

International terrorism is on the increase, and religious conflicts are taking an alarming toll in terms of human lives and property losses. Human rights violations have become common, involving governments, religious, and political organizations.

The crude oil price, after a series of roller-coaster fluctuations, has finally crashed, subsequently causing world trade and money market instability. This has also resulted in massive "lay-offs" of workers from major local and multinational organizations worldwide. Unemployment rate has increased, inflicting pressure on people's earnings, as well as on healthcare. Unsurprisingly, suicide rates have increased both among the young and the old.

Sexual perversion has also increased tremendously, and marriages are becoming increasingly unstable. A remarkable number of "men of God" have fallen into fornication and adultery. Churches and other religious organizations openly endorse unethical and reckless political groups. This is indeed an irony, as it seems people now tend to accept wrong unethical conducts to be the norm.

Racial and tribal discriminations have resulted in massive immigration problems, and refugees are increasingly angry and desperate in their hopelessness. The "Mother Earth" also seems to be equally upset as it issues out several natural disasters, including volcanic eruptions, earthquakes, severe and higher categories of hurricanes, tornadoes, tropical storms, landslides, mudslides, excessive flooding and the likes – leading to massive devastations and extensive loss of lives.

This indeed is the right time to address the trend of unrest worldwide. The question is, where can one find rest in this restless world?

ULTIMATE RESTING PLACE

The ultimate and true place to find rest is in the divine bosom of the Lord. No matter how things may be around us, if we come to the Lord, He will give us rest for our souls. He invites all in Matthew 11:28-30, saying, "Come to Me, all you who labor and are heavy laden, and I will give you rest. Take My yoke upon you and learn from Me, for I am gentle and lowly in heart, and you will find rest for your souls. For My yoke is easy and My burden is light."

Jesus' words recall a statement made by personified wisdom in a Jewish document dating to several hundred years before Christ. When combined with Matthew 11:19, this suggests that Jesus portrayed Himself as personified wisdom, the One who exists eternally and acted on Yahweh's behalf to create the world (1 Corinthians 1:24; Matthew 11:16-19). Jesus' teaching provided an easy yoke, in contrast to the heavy suppressive yoke of rabbinic teaching (Matthew 23:4; Acts 5:10). By identifying Himself with personified wisdom, Jesus hinted that He is the eternal One through whom the Father created everything (John 1:3).

In Matthew 6:25-34, Jesus talks at length about the importance of not stressing or worrying over the various issues of life. He says, "Therefore I say to you, do not worry about your life, what you will eat or what you will drink; nor about your body, what you will put on. Is not life more than food and the body more than clothing?..." The rabbinic–style argument reasons that if God does a greater thing for us, He will also do lesser things. Specifically, if God created you (the greater accomplishment), He is certainly capable of feeding you (a lesser accomplishment).

It is not God's will that you live in a state of worry. He has got your back and will never let you down. Surrender to Him faithfully, trust in Him, live in confidence and assurance and you will enjoy such rest every day that the world cannot find or fathom. In Matthew 6:33-34 Jesus says, "But seek first the kingdom of God and His righteousness, and all these things shall be added to you. Therefore do not worry about tomorrow, for tomorrow will worry about its own things. Sufficient for the day is its own trouble."

Worry is futile and cannot prolong your life. Jesus revealed that the real cause of anxiety is when we have little faith, or more precisely, when we doubt God's power and desire to provide for His children. The disciple who values the reign of God over his life and who diligently pursues righteous living can trust God to satisfy his needs. Obsession with material possessions displays the warped priorities of Gentiles (Colossians 3:5). Jesus does not prohibit planning for the future, but He does prohibit worrying about it. He urges believers instead to focus on the challenges of the present.

COMMON CAUSES OF RESTLESSNESS

1. Anxiety (Luke 12:29-30). This could be triggered by unstable socio-political climate, financial insecurity, uncertain future, old age and so on.

2. Fear (Joshua 5:1). This includes fear for personal safety, or fear of injurious aspects of government-imposed law and order.

3. Sinfulness (Isaiah 48:22). Wickedness, ungodly lifestyles and the likes are perpetual causes of restlessness.

4. Divisions and strife (Psalm 67:7; Proverbs 17:1)

5. Stress (Psalm 127:2). This could be caused by sickness, personal tragedies, loss of income, etc.

6. Greed (Ecclesiastes 4:6).

KEYS TO FINDING REST

1. Speak words of peace and encouragement daily. It is rewarding to keep on speaking words of peace and encouragement over yourself daily, while also encouraging and speaking life to others under all circumstances. 1 Samuel 30:6 says, "Now David was greatly distressed, for the people spoke of stoning him, because the soul of all the people was grieved, every man for his sons and his daughters. But David strengthened himself in the Lord his God."

"David strengthened himself in the Lord his God" reveals a testimony to his faith in difficult times. Those who sow stress will reap stress, but those who reap peace will reap good. Isaiah 50:4 states, "The Lord God has given Me The tongue of the learned, that I should know how to speak a word in season to him who is weary. He awakens me morning by morning, He awakens my ear to hear as the learned."

The speaker above is a student of God, trained to provide encouragement to those who are weary. Each morning God awakens Him with new insight. James

3:18 also says, "Now the fruit of righteousness is sown in peace by those who make peace." James explained that teachers who teach on the basis of "earthly wisdom" produce confusion and every evil thing. Conversely, teachers who possess wisdom from above produce virtues that fulfill the "royal law". (James 2:8). Attitudes among Christians should be based on the royal law, which says love your neighbor as yourself (Leviticus 19:18; Matthew 19:19; 22:39). Favoritism violates this command, thus convicting those guilty of its practice as transgressors of the law.

2. Let God be your confidence and provider. You will not live in stress or anxiety if you let God be your confidence and provider (Proverbs 3:26; Isaiah 26:3). Proverbs 3:26 assures, "For the Lord will be your confidence, and will keep your foot from being caught." Though the wicked will suddenly come to trouble at their ending (Psalm 35:8), those who maintain wisdom (Proverbs 3:21) will never be in such danger – whether up and about or sleeping – because the Lord will protect them.

Believers should trust God completely and solely, never relying on our ability or anyone else's. Jeremiah 17:7-8 says, "Blessed is the man who trusts in the Lord, and whose hope is the Lord. For he shall be like a tree planted by the waters, which spreads out its roots by the river, and will not fear when heat comes; But its leaf will be green, and will not be anxious in the year of drought, nor will cease from yielding fruit." It is equally vital for us to steadily keep our faith and trust in God as a priority. Our faith is the victory that overcomes the world (1 John 5:4). We need to involve God in everything we do and make Him part of our daily life (1 Corinthians 3:9). We are God's friends, co-workers, and our work with Him extends far beyond the walls of the church into everything we do daily – indeed, all aspects of our lives.

3. Watch what you hear. Contemporary media outlets have become the most paramount sources of misinformation to the public. This requires you to be extra cautious. You must watch what you are listening to, and be sure to listen to the Spirit of God more than the voice of men. Peace and rest are found in the voice of God's spirit speaking to us (Luke 8:18).

The Holy Spirit living inside us has an answer for every circumstance of life. Jesus, in John 14:26-27, states, "But the Helper, the Holy Spirit, whom the Father will send in My name, He will teach you all things, and bring to your remembrance all things that I said to you. Peace I leave with you, My peace I give to you; not as the world gives do I give to you. Let not your heart be troubled, neither let it be afraid."

God has given us the gift of His everlasting peace,

and we must learn to tune out of the noise that comes from the outside (media, social networks, friends and associates and so on), as well as the strange voices, wandering thoughts and negative thinking that arise from all these unstable sources of information in the restless world.

4. Be patient and tenacious in your faith. Give no place to doubt and unbelief in your dealings with God and His word. Hebrews 6:11-12 exhorts believers, "And we desire that each one of you show the same diligence to the full assurance of hope until the end, that you do not become sluggish, but imitate those who through faith and patience inherit the promises."

God expects believers to progress toward maturity and show diligence in their faith and unwavering patience. We are to follow the example of Abraham, who obtained the promise of God after he had patiently endured, and we should lay hold of the hope before us because God has confirmed His promise with an oath.

The Christian has a sure and firm anchor of the soul because Jesus has entered the inner sanctuary of God's presence. There is not a hint of wavering in God's will or the final outcome for His dear friends. Cast your burdens on Jesus, and do not try to carry them by yourself, since this is already assured in scriptures (Matthew 11:28-30; 1 Peter 5:7).

Instead of fretting or worrying about any problem, pray about it, stay united with other believers, and be joyful. Philippians 4:6-7 encourages us thus, "Be anxious for nothing, but in everything by prayer and supplication, with thanksgiving, let your requests be made known to God; and the peace of God, which surpasses all understanding, will guard your hearts and minds through Christ Jesus." "Anxious" refers to worry (Matthew 6:25-34).

Prayer is the antidote to anxiety. Three words express different aspects of prayer: Prayer, a worshipful attitude; supplication, need; and request, the specific concern. Thanksgiving shapes prayers with gratitude. In response, the peace of God brings power to endure. The peace calms down a troubling situation when explanations fail. Further, peace guards by keeping anxieties from hearts (choices) and minds (attitudes).

5. Know that victory is assured (whatever happens). A believer's victory is so well ultimately assured that even death cannot overcome you, because then, you go to glory to be with God. Hallelujah! Jesus has conquered Satan and death finally. Christ has already overcome the world.

2 Corinthians 2:14 says, "Now thanks be to God who always leads us in triumph in Christ, and through us diffuses the fragrance of His knowledge in every

place." Here, Christ is leading Paul and all other believers into the eternal city where God is King, a portrayal of triumph in Christ.

Be reminded gain that God has got your back at all times – so you have no reason to be desperate. Hebrews 13:5-6 says, "Let your conduct be without covetousness; be content with such things as you have. For He Himself has said, "I will never leave you nor forsake you." So we may boldly say: "The Lord is my helper; I will not fear. What can man do to me?"

BECOMING THE SPIRIT'S RESTING PLACE

Since the time of Pentecost, the Holy Spirit has been seeking for people He can dwell in as His resting place. No demonic power can block the fellowship of the Spirit of God in us and the Father in heaven because He dwells in us. Besides, we are operating under open heavens! And may we ever be the resting place for the Spirit and the power of God in the mighty name of Jesus Christ.

It is indeed a great supplication as we often pray that God rend the heavens, come down and cause His will to be established over our environment. However, in as much as this is an excellent prayer, we are praying in ignorance because the sovereign God has already opened the heavens. Incidentally, Isaiah prayed a similar prayer; but it was necessary in his case because the Holy Spirit had not yet been given. This was what Isaiah was yearning for. Isaiah 64:1 says, "Oh, that You would rend the heavens! That You would come down! That the mountains might shake at Your presence."

We find the answer to this supplication in Matthew 3:16-17, which says, "When He had been baptized, Jesus came up immediately from the water; and behold, the heavens were opened to Him, and He saw the Spirit of God descending like a dove and alighting upon Him. And suddenly a voice came from heaven, saying, "This is My beloved Son, in whom I am well pleased." As the Scripture says, at Christ's baptism, the heavens were opened and the Holy Spirit came down and "rested" upon Jesus and, since then, the open heavens have remained so.

The opening of the heavens demonstrates that both the voice and the descending Spirit came from heaven and were divine. First century Jews associated the dove with the Spirit, since Genesis 1:2 describes the Spirit as "hovering" over primeval waters. The Hebrew verb used in the passage is the same word used to describe a bird fluttering its wings (Deuteronomy 32:11). The descent of the Spirit thus alludes to Genesis 1 and identified Jesus as One who brings new creation (2 Corinthians 5:17; Galatians 6:15).

DWELLING PLACE VS. RESTING PLACE

Let us examine what it really means to become the resting place for the Spirit of God. For this to happen, we must allow and facilitate hosting of the presence of God in our soul and around all that we render in our entire life. The goal is for us all to learn to host the presence of God, since the Holy Spirit lives in every believer but does not rest on every believer.

When the Spirit rests upon us, every place we go or appear, the atmosphere changes when we show up. Hosting the presence of God in our body means becoming the resting place for the Spirit of God, so much that He finds expression in our daily living – healing the sick, raising the dead, and putting demons to flight.

God has revealed to us that it is possible for us to give Him a resting place in our body to the extent that things shift or change in a room simply because we stepped into that room. The following are examples of people who made themselves available as the resting place for the Holy Spirit, as well as the evidence of such Spirit hosting:

1. Jesus Christ – as seen in the case of the woman with the issue of blood and many other miracles (Luke 8:43-48).

2. Apostle Peter – as revealed by the beautiful gate experience and His shadow healing people (Acts 3:1-10).

3. Apostle Paul – as demonstrated in his apron driving away demons, miles away from him (Acts 19:11-12).

To be like the people mentioned above and many others whom the Holy Spirit rested on with attendant wonders, observe the following:

1. Learn to always cooperate with the Holy Spirit in your ministry – everything outside the work of the Holy Spirit in you is vain effort.

2. Believe that God has called you to heal the sick, raise the dead and cast out demons – Matthew 10:8.

3. Be conscious of the presence of God/Holy Spirit always because what you are conscious of, you are able to possess, manifest and or/release – 1 John 4:4; Hebrews 13:5.

4. Realize the ministry of the gospel is not just a ministry of words – it is a ministry of releasing the presence of God into the atmosphere.

5. Realize that when you say what God is saying, you impart His presence with your words. If you tap into the heart of the Father, through impartation, something is released to the atmosphere as you speak.

6. Realize that whatever overshadows you will manifest through your shadow. What you host, what your affections are anchored on are things you will manifest – 2 Corinthians 6:12 says you are restricted by your affections.

7. No matter what the circumstances are, JUST DO IT!

Let's observe again that faith comes by surrender, not by either determination or exercise of an extraordinary will power. Faith comes not out of rest whereby you choose to rest in God; in other words, faith does not come out of dissipation of energy or out of efforts. Counterfeit faith is created by striving to do, but with rest, faith manifests as a normal expression of the believer's daily life.

CHAPTER 7
PATIENCE IS STILL GOLDEN

Patience is a vibrant and virile Christian virtue, which is deeply rooted in the Christian's absolute confidence in the sovereignty of God and in God's promise to bring all things to completion in a way that most fully demonstrates His glory. —Albert Mohler

It is apparent nowadays in public places and on social media that people demonstrate an increasing degree of impatience with one another. The good "old school" decorum and respect maintained in earlier times are fast disappearing. People are much more suspicious of one another, and there seems to be no modicum of public friendly disposition.

Even as terrorist activities and religious unrests escalate globally, people are no longer comfortable with safety precautions, particularly in public places. They no longer trust government to provide necessary security measures. Indeed, globally, people, as well as various national governments, have become grossly impatient with one another.

WHAT PATIENCE IS

Patience is active endurance of delay, discomfort or opposition. It does not connote passive resignation. As James 1:4 says, "But let patience have its perfect work, that you may be perfect and complete, lacking nothing." Patience indicates that further work must be done for the purpose of making the believer perfect and complete. The opposites - immaturity and incompletion - are not acceptable long-term states for the Christian disciple.

God is patient (Romans 15:5) and slow to anger (Psalm 102:8). Romans 15:5-6 says, "Now may the God of patience and comfort grant you to be like-minded toward one another, according to Christ Jesus, that you may with one mind and one mouth glorify the God and Father of our Lord Jesus Christ."

Apostle Paul's prayer is that God will bring these house churches of Rome to the place of harmony, love, and unity that will enable them to best honor God. Christian love is patient (1 Corinthians 13:4, 7). As Christians, we must be patient and endure in the face of persecution. We need endurance, rather than shrinking back during adversity (Hebrews 6:9-15; 10:32-39).

Jesus is our great example of endurance (Hebrews 12:1-3). David learned to be patient with the prosperity of the wicked (Psalm 37:1-3; 9-13, 34-38). We too need to learn to face adversity with patience (Romans 5:3-5).

WHAT PATIENCE IS NOT

The Church, in general, has consistently misunderstood what patience is by misquoting Romans 8:28 when bad things happen to some people. Romans 8:28 says, "And we know that all things work together for good to those who love God, to those who are the called according to His purpose."

Church people often use this to justify every tragic event the devil brings on people. This is very wrong. For instance, if a child dies prematurely by an unknown cause, they use the same text to console, as if God is the cause of the disaster. Our Lord is good all the time (Psalm 136:1) and His mercies endure forever. The right and correct application of Romans 8:28, in this context, is to identify the culprit (the devil), resist him, and he will flee. As James 4:7 says, "Therefore submit to God. Resist the devil and he will flee from you."

To "submit to God" carries the idea of self-humbling;

while "resist the devil" suggests an active resistance against temptation. But in the process of misapplying patience, believers surrender in ignorance to the devil's wickedness, as in Job's case, claiming (in error) that the Lord gives and takes away (Job 1:21).

The right attitude for believers is to base our patience on the word of God, rather than quitting or surrendering.

TEMPLATES OF PATIENCE

1. God's patience. Romans 2:4-5 says, "Or do you despise the riches of His goodness, forbearance, and longsuffering, not knowing that the goodness of God leads you to repentance? But in accordance with your hardness and your impenitent heart you are treasuring up for yourself wrath in the day of wrath and revelation of the righteous judgment of God." God is patient, but His patience does not mean that He condones evil. There is certainly an appointed time of judgment for the unrepentant (Romans 14:10; Revelation 20:11-15). The wise course is to settle your case with God before then (Matthew 5:25-26).

Like water pooling behind a dam, individuals and societies accumulate a debt of wrath as they continue to reject God's grace. God demonstrated extreme patience dealing with the Israelites, and also with us at the present age. 1 Peter 3:20 states, "Who formerly were disobedient, when once the Divine longsuffering waited in the days of Noah, while the ark was being prepared, in which a few, that is, eight souls, were saved through water." God's patience is purposeful. While Noah and his family were saved through water, or brought safely through the floodwaters, the wicked were destroyed by the same water (Genesis 7:22-23). God's longsuffering caused Him to wait patiently for Noah to build the ark, just to save eight souls.

2. Patience is wisdom. When we are slow to wrath, we are able to rethink our actions and act wisely. Proverbs 14:29 says, "He who is slow to wrath has great understanding, but he who is impulsive exalts folly."

3. Patience is an aspect of faith and hope. Abraham waited for the promised child for 25 years; he did not waver but trusted strongly in the Lord. Romans 4:18-21 says, "who, contrary to hope, in hope believed, so that he became the father of many nations, according to what was spoken, "So shall your descendants be." And not being weak in faith, he did not consider his own body, already dead (since he was about a hundred years old), and the deadness of Sarah's womb. He did not waver at the promise of God through unbelief, but was strengthened in faith, giving glory to God, and being fully convinced that what He had promised He was also able to perform." Acts 1:4 also states, "And being assembled together with them, He commanded them not to depart from Jerusalem, but to wait for the Promise of the Father, "which," He said, "you have heard from Me." The Father's promise refers to the gift of the Holy Spirit, which was soon to come (Acts 2); but the disciples needed to patiently wait in prayer and expectation to obtain the promise.

4. Patience leads to righteousness. We are able to reap good harvests in due season when we demonstrate patience, based on the word of God. Galatians 6:9 says, "And let us not grow weary while doing good, for in due season we shall reap if we do not lose heart." Since the Christian life is a marathon race, we must be patient, persevere, and must not grow weary or lose heart. Doing good is not seeking to be justified by works, but living as ordained by God for those who have received His gracious salvation through faith (Ephesians 2:8-10).

5. Patience is part of fruit of the Spirit. We can influence our environment more by the fruit that we manifest than by any evangelism we do in hypocrisy. By people's fruits, you shall definitely read and know them. Galatians 5:22-23 states, "But the fruit of the Spirit is love, joy, peace, longsuffering [patience], kindness, goodness, faithfulness, gentleness, self-control. Against such there is no law." Illustration of fruit hints on the vine and branches that produce fruit. The love here is such loving behavior coming through the power of the Holy Spirit by faith. Self-control is placed last to emphasize the fact that all the works of the flesh reflect lack of self-control.

6. Patience helps us to achieve perfection. We are able to turn adversity into positive growth with patience. James 1:2-4 says, "My brethren, count it all joy when you fall into various trials, knowing that the testing of your faith produces patience. But let patience have its perfect work, that you may be perfect and complete, lacking nothing." The use of the word "when" and not "if" denotes that trials are normal part of the Christian life, and are a given for a faithful disciple (2 Timothy 3:12).

The joy with which a believer endures trials in the present is a sign of their hope for future relief. Knowledge that trials produce patience is the basis for joy. Patience is the ability to persevere through increasing levels of testing or suffering. Patience also hints that further work must be done for the purpose of making the believer perfect and complete.

7. Christ patiently waited for Saul to become Paul. Jesus Christ demonstrated patience as he waited for Saul to eventually repent and become Paul. Paul gave his testimony in 1 Timothy 1:16, "However, for this reason I obtained mercy, that in me first Jesus Christ might show all longsuffering, as a pattern to those who are going to believe on Him for everlasting life."

Paul's sudden transformation was not due to his own faithfulness or his ignorance, and he marveled at his conversion since he knew himself to be so bad. He was an example of what true salvation was supposed to accomplish. He was the sort of person for whom the law was intended (1 Timothy 1:9-10). The result of the gospel in his life was not idle speculation but transformation.

8. Patience is a characteristic of love. Love is patient and involves all ramifications of patience. The discord, tumult and divorces plaguing marriages will be minimized if only we demonstrate adequate tolerance and levels of patience with one another. 1 Corinthians 13:4-7 tells us, "Love suffers long and is kind; love does not envy; love does not parade itself, is not puffed up; does not behave rudely, does not seek its own, is not provoked, thinks no evil; does not rejoice in iniquity, but rejoices in the truth; bears all things, believes all things, hopes all things, endures all things." Here, Paul personifies love in order to show its daily character and choices.

9. Patience leads to trust in the Lord. People who possess the true virtue of patience bear challenges and trials of life calmly, no matter how severe and seemingly hopeless the situation may appear. God wants us to stand like a rock in the face of adversity. King Saul failed the test of patience, unfortunately, and hence lost the throne. Psalm 27:14 says, "Wait on the Lord; be of good courage, and He shall strengthen your heart; Wait, I say, on the Lord!" Rather than taking matters into our hands, we must learn to wait patiently for Yahweh's response to our prayers (Psalm 37:7, 40:1; Proverbs 20:22).

YES, PATIENCE PAYS!

We can consciously avoid the unwarranted penalties and hassles associated with impatience - such as high blood pressure, heart attack, anger, anxiety, impulsive attitudes, increased frustrations and strained relationships. The key is to optimistically endure difficult circumstances, regarding them just as a passing phase.

The process of our patience may not necessarily cause our problems to disappear overnight, but can make the delays bearable. Patience is much more than the outward action of waiting; it involves an inner mental interactive attitude that helps us to be calm and well-disposed, rather than being annoyed and paranoid while we wait.

CHAPTER 8

HEARING THE VOICE OF GOD

We should ever aim at coming into contact with God in the morning, so that hearing His voice we may be made conscious of His presence, and know the inspiration that comes from such a meeting. —Duncan Campbell

The cliché "no news is good news" seems to be more relevant nowadays when most of the information released on the Internet and social media is horror news. This is also branded as "breaking news" - always alerting the public of strange, fearful and repulsive events that may still be pending confirmation by some other more reliable media. The global socio-economic, political, religious, and cultural environments continue to be plagued by these negative reports. Essentially, it has become unprofitable to pay much attention to media and social news, as people's minds are being manipulated and beclouded by various interest groups.

Added to this media malaise is the inordinate craving for money that has become so rampant nowadays, afflicting both the young and the old. Yet, in all of these, God continues to speak to us – to guide, instruct, correct, advice, assure and caution. Sadly, however, the majority of us are not listening.

God made us for Himself, and He wants our fellowship with Him to be uninterrupted. Revelation 4:11 says, "You are worthy, O Lord, To receive glory and honor and power; for You created all things, and by Your will they exist and were created." Communication is a crucial aspect of every relationship, and therefore a critical proof of our oneness with God. We must, therefore, remain in constant communication with Him.

The heavenly throne of God is characterized by unceasing joyful praise, thanksgiving, and worship toward the Lord by the four living creatures and the twenty-four elders. The beginning point of worship is to recognize that God is completely worthy to be recognized for His unrivaled glory and honor and power, and His work as Creator and sustainer of all things.

Jesus, the Good Shepherd, states as follows in John 10:27-28, "My sheep hear My voice, and I know them, and they follow Me. And I give them eternal life, and they shall never perish; neither shall anyone snatch them out of My hand." It is of vital importance for believers to recognize and maintain constant communion with God always. He has given us the gift of the Holy Spirit so we can link up with Him anytime for help and for direct communication and relationship.

PATTERN OF COMMUNION BETWEEN GOD AND MAN

Communication between God and man had been regular, constant and perfect before the fall in the Garden of Eden. Genesis 3:8-10 states, "And they heard the sound of the Lord God walking in the garden in the cool of the day, and Adam and his wife hid themselves from the presence of the Lord God among the trees of the garden. Then the Lord God called to Adam and said to him, "Where are you?" So he said, "I heard Your voice in the garden, and I was afraid because I was naked; and I hid myself."

Even after the fall, God, in His unfailing mercy and grace, took the initiative in reaching out to sinful humanity, which becomes the primary theme of the rest of the Bible. Its ultimate expression is found in Jesus Christ who came to save the people alienated from God because of their sin (Luke 19:10). In Him God once again walked on earth in search of sinners. The omniscient (all-knowing) God had previously asked Adam, "Where are you?" to encourage him to face his sin.

Moreover, with the coming of Jesus, the Good Shepherd, God expects us, being His sheep, to hear His voice, rather than the voice of strangers, the devil and his agents (John 10:1-6). John 10:4-5 says, "And when he brings out his own sheep, he goes before them; and the sheep follow him, for they know his voice. Yet they will by no means follow a stranger, but will flee from him, for they do not know the voice of strangers." Not only is Jesus the Good Shepherd, He is also the door through which believers find abundant, eternal life (John 10:9-10).

It is also worth noting that, long before Pentecost, the Holy Spirit had rested on particular individuals on specific assignments. For instance, Numbers 11:26 says, "But two men had remained in the camp: the name of one was Eldad, and the name of the other Medad. And the Spirit rested upon them. Now they were among those listed, but who had not gone out to the tabernacle; yet they prophesied in the camp."

Two elders, Eldad and Medad, who had not attended the presentation ceremony organized by Moses on God's instruction, prophesied in the same manner as the other elders, demonstrating that God's Spirit cannot be confined to any space or time. He longs to have communion with as many as are willing to let Him have His way in their lives.

In 2 Kings 2:15, we are told, "Now when the sons of the prophets who were from Jericho saw him, they said, "The spirit of Elijah rests on Elisha." And they came to meet him, and bowed to the ground before him." Elijah's mantle showed that Elisha was the legitimate heir, and the mantle was a concrete symbol of God's power to the watchers. The coming of the Holy Spirit was demonstrated on Pentecost (Acts 2). More cheeringly now, the Holy Spirit rests on every believer - unlike before Pentecost when the Holy Spirit only rested on particular individuals as shown above. Acts 2:1-2 says, "When the Day of Pentecost had fully come, they were all with one accord in one place. And suddenly there came a sound from heaven, as of a rushing mighty wind, and it filled the whole house where they were sitting. Then there appeared to them divided tongues, as of fire, and one sat upon each of them. And they were all filled with the Holy Spirit and began to speak with other tongues, as the Spirit gave them utterance."

The events of Pentecost marked the formal public beginning of the church that involved a number of natural phenomena. These included rush of violent wind from heaven, tongues like flame of fire, the infilling with the Holy Spirit, and speaking in languages as the Spirit gave believers ability to do so.

DEEPER REVELATIONS

Now that the Holy Spirit resides in us, to hear the voice of God, we should be listening inside us to detect and hear the voice of the Spirit. 1 Corinthians 6:17 says, "But he who is joined to the Lord is one spirit with Him." Here, Paul tells believers in Corinth to remember the oneness and sanctity of their union with Christ, and must glorify God in body and spirit.

As born-again Christians, we must know that "God is Spirit, and those who worship Him must worship in spirit and truth." (John 4:24) We must also know that each of us too is a spirit, having a soul and living in a body. The Israelites were instructed not to make idols or the likeness of anything - as the surrounding nations did (Exodus 20:4) – because, undoubtedly, God is Spirit. Proper worship of God is a matter of spirit, rather than physical location.

1 Thessalonians 5:23-24 also states, "Now may the God of peace Himself sanctify you completely; and may your whole spirit, soul, and body be preserved blameless at the coming of our Lord Jesus Christ. He who calls you is faithful, who also will do it." This is in blessing and admonition, the prayer for the spirit, soul, and body to be kept sound and blameless. It explains that God sees the whole person as important in living a life pleasing to God.

HOW TO HEAR FROM GOD

1. Declutter from busyness. You need to declutter your life from busyness. Luke 10:41-42 says, "And Jesus answered and said to her, "Martha, Martha, you are worried and troubled about many things. But one thing is needed, and Mary has chosen that good part, which will not be taken away from her."

Martha was distracted from what should have been her highest priority – learning from Jesus. She was full of care and troubled about household chores that needed to be done, and she was irritated with her sister Mary because it was the role of women to serve men at such a setting. Jesus indicated that Martha's focus should be the same as her sister's – discipleship, an eternally commendable choice that will never be taken away.

2. Do not be conformed to the world. Die to the world and fix your mind on things above. 1 John 2:15-17 states, "Do not love the world or the things in the world. If anyone loves the world, the love of the Father is not in him. For all that is in the world—the lust of the flesh, the lust of the eyes, and the pride of life—is not of the Father but is of the world. And the world is passing away, and the lust of it; but he who does the will of God abides forever." Things associated with the world are not just material objects, but things that absorb human love for the Father to an undue degree, even to the point of supplanting God from the mind (John 5:21).

3. Abide in Christ, the true vine. Be connected to Jesus, as the vine and its branches. In John 15:1-8, Jesus says, "I am the true vine, and My Father is the vinedresser. Every branch in Me that does not bear fruit He takes away; and every branch that bears fruit He prunes, that it may bear more fruit…Abide in Me, and I in you. As the branch cannot bear fruit of itself, unless it abides in the vine, neither can you, unless you abide in Me… If you abide in Me, and My words abide in you, you will ask what you desire, and it shall be done for you. By this My Father is glorified, that you bear much fruit; so you will be My disciples."

The Father (God) is depicted as the vinedresser, while the true vine is Jesus. To ensure maximal fruit production, the divine vineyard keeper removes dead branches and prunes all the others (Hebrew 6:7-8). Judas, the betrayer, is an example of a dead branch (John 13:10-11), while Peter is an example of a living branch, despite denying the Lord thrice at the initial moment (John 18:15-18, 25-27; 21:15-19).

4. Rely on the Holy Spirit inside you. The Holy Spirit in you is the ultimate helper to ask for assistance to accomplish tasks. 1 Corinthians 3:16-17 says, "Do you not know that you are the temple of God and that the Spirit of God dwells in you? If anyone defiles the temple of God, God will destroy him. For the temple of God is holy, which temple you are." The ultimate identity of believers' corporate body (as well as the physical) must be reverenced always as we are a temple built by God.

5. Familiarize yourself with the word. It is essential that believers spend time on the word of God. A major hindrance to strong faith is lack of the word – a non-excuse for believers. God instructs in Joshua 1:8, "This Book of the Law shall not depart from your mouth, but you shall meditate in it day and night, that you may observe to do according to all that is written in it. For then you will make your way prosperous, and then you will have good success." Studying and learning from the word of God are to form so much a part of our lives that the words are fully obeyed (as in Deuteronomy 6:6-9). God's promised presence in Joshua 1:5,9 indicates that Joshua's success will come because God is with him, enabling him to read and observe God's word (Ephesians 2:8-10)

CHANNELS OF HEARING FROM GOD

- His word – 2 Timothy 3:16
- The Holy Spirit – John 14:26
- The still small voice within us - 1 Corinthians 6:17 (We need to slow down to hear, Psalm 46:10)

- Through the Son, the living Word – Hebrews 1:1-2
- Lessons from the troubles of our lives – Psalm 119:67
- Inner impressions – Romans 8:16
- Anointed teaching and fellowship – Amos 3:7; 1 Thessalonians 2:13; 1 Corinthians 2:13

BENEFITS OF HEARING FROM GOD

1. Only God knows the correct way. Isaiah 30:21 says, "Your ears shall hear a word behind you, saying, "This is the way, walk in it," Whenever you turn to the right hand or whenever you turn to the left." Walking in the way is reminiscent of the language of Psalm 1. There are two ways defined - a crooked path that represents an evil way, heading towards death; and the straight path of godliness that leads to life.

2. Hearing God prevents us from making unnecessary mistakes. Proverbs 14:12 warns, "There is a way that seems right to a man, but its end is the way of death." The ultimate result of a wrong choice is death, which should be avoided by making right decisions through God's guidance.

3. Hearing God and doing what He wants us to do gives us rest that our lives are on track, and that we

are not wasting it. Jesus reveals the disappointment that many will face on the day of judgment: "And then I will declare to them, 'I never knew you; depart from Me, you who practice lawlessness!'" (Matthew 7:23). Jesus reveals here that a person is confirmed to be a true disciple not by prophecy or working of miracles but by living a transformed life made possible by God. The disobedient lifestyles of evildoers are inconsistent with genuine discipleship. Jesus' words, "I never knew you" show that these were never truly disciples.

4. Hearing from God removes doubts and unbelief and solidifies our faith, preventing us from wavering. Of Abraham, Romans 4:20-21 states, "He did not waver at the promise of God through unbelief, but was strengthened in faith, giving glory to God, and being fully convinced that what He had promised He was also able to perform." Abraham had realistic evaluation of his prospects for fatherhood. Yet Abraham did not doubt God's promise, and God strengthened his faith.

5. Hearing from God validates our relationship with Him. Since hearing from God proves that we are His sheep, not hearing from Him is a sign that we are not of Him. Jesus, says in John 10:2-3, "But he who enters by the door is the shepherd of the sheep. To him the doorkeeper opens, and the sheep

hear his voice; and he calls his own sheep by name and leads them out."

It should be emphasized that, communication is a very crucial aspect of believers' relationship with God. Unfortunately, there are way too many hindrances to hearing God's voice caused by the worries of daily life. Believers must learn to focus and listen to their inner man, to always connect with the Spirit and hear the voice of God. God is always speaking. We are the ones not listening.

CHAPTER 9
KNOWLEDGE IS POWER

Knowledge is indispensable to Christian life and service. If we do not use the mind that God has given us, we condemn ourselves to spiritual superficiality and cut ourselves off from many of the riches of God's grace.
—John Stott

Knowledge involves acquaintance with facts, truths, or principles as from a study or an investigation. It is an embodiment of truths or facts that are historically accumulated in the course of time. Performance of any accomplishment in life must be preceded by an adequate knowledge on aspects of such a thing. Business literature refers to this as the essence of the value of information.

As a science lecturer currently in the university, the regular issues some of my students raise are about high costs of lecture and lab books published for modern-style education. The books are interactive and informative in all ramifications, as well as being loaded with real life color captions and photographs. I usually try to remind the students that it is better to pay for the high cost of education than risk the danger of ignorance.

Regarding the consequence of ignorance, God said of the Israelites in Hosea 4:6, "My people are destroyed for lack of knowledge. Because you have rejected knowledge, I also will reject you from being priest for Me; Because you have forgotten the law of your God, I also will forget your children." Due to lack of the knowledge of God, the people had ceased to care about knowing Him or the truth about Him (Romans 1:18-32). As a result they were violating the Ten Commandments and suffering the consequences.

The common people are identified as guilty, but especially guilty were the priests who were responsible for teaching the people. Leaders of God's people who shirk or violate that responsibility invite special punishment (Malachi 2:1-9; Matthew 18:6; James 3:1). We must remove obstacles that tend to prevent the growth of our faith, such as lack of time and knowledge, due to worldly busyness. Other hindrances may arise from lack of knowledge and understanding of our new creation, our righteousness, our place in Christ Jesus, failure regarding the privilege to use the name of Jesus, lack of confession, and acting on the Word of God like it is true!

KNOWLEDGE AS FAITH-BOOSTER

Knowledge serves to enhance our faith in two major ways:

1. Knowledge of God's word. Knowledge of what God has said emboldens us to approach the Throne of Grace with our requests. It also helps to solidify our faith in God's omnipotence. The average word-informed (word-acknowledgeable) believer would, for instance, respond to what God has said about sickness and disease. 1 Peter 2:24 says, "Who Himself bore our sins in His own body on the tree, that we, having died to sins, might live for righteousness—by whose stripes you were healed."

By Christ's death, believers are healed spiritually. I am a living testimony of this kind of spiritual healing, which occurred in year 2,000, when I was miraculously healed of a hip joint arthritis ailment. A couple of years earlier, I had been scheduled to undergo surgical operation on both my right and left hip joints, badly damaged by rheumatoid arthritis. I had not really understood this healing scripture by the time I underwent the first surgical operation for my left hip joint, which was scheduled to be complemented by the second operation on the supposed equally bad right hip. The physicians (rheumatologists) recommended I should allow a six-month interval to perform the second surgical operation of the right hip.

While going through the recovery process on my hospital bed, my Pastor more rigorously admonished me on 1 Peter 2:24 (and Isaiah 53:5). I trained to meditate so effectively on this scripture, until I imagined it constantly working spiritually in my soul, and I subsequently received physical healing manifestation. By the grace of our faithful God, I never went back for the proposed second hip surgical operation. I have been healed by His stripes! And it's been 18 years thereafter with no symptom. Hallelujah! Glory to God!!

About our needs being met, our response, based on scriptural knowledge, would be "all my needs are supplied according to His riches in glory", paraphrased from Philippians 4:19 which says, "And my God shall supply all your need according to His riches in glory by Christ Jesus." And, on prosperity, 3 John 1:2 says, "Beloved, I pray that you may prosper in all things and be in health, just as your soul prospers."

We generally agree and feel faith would work automatically if we could get enough knowledge about what God has said about angels, demons, Holy Spirit, prayer, health, prosperity, and faith.

2. Knowledge of the faithfulness of God: Faith is built on the knowledge of the reliability and trustworthiness of the character of the One who gives His word or makes a promise! We generally lack this knowledge in our faith walk. Some believers have absolutely no knowledge of God's reliability because they do everything in their abilities. They use their own wisdom for issues of life, since they lack information about the character of God or His trustworthiness.

Believers must appreciate God's faithfulness and the fact that He can be counted on to do whatever He says He will do in His word! Hebrews 11:11-12 says, "By faith Sarah herself also received strength to conceive seed, and she bore a child when she was past the age, because she judged Him faithful who had promised. Therefore from one man, and him as good as dead, were born as many as the stars of the sky in multitude—innumerable as the sand which is by the seashore."

This is an illustration that is unique in the Bible – of someone who went from zero, faith-wise, to become a person who is included in the "Hall of Fame" of heroes of faith. She tracked from zero faith-level to the point of exercising great faith, while most believers simply assume that God will do what He says He will do simply because He is God.

The pertinent question, therefore, is: How much knowledge do we have experientially about God's reliability and trustworthiness about what He has said and promised? We can only have that knowledge as we walk by faith and actually apply the word to our lives. Every believer can see the promises of God come to pass in his life if he will take time to meditate on who he is in Christ and what he has in Christ, and be sincere to act like God's word is true!

NEED FOR FAITH REAWAKENING

Christians in general actually appear to have slowed down, instead of being quicker to always act on the word of God. Our case seems to be different from that of the Thessalonians, of whom Paul wrote: "We are bound to thank God always for you, brethren, as it is fitting, because your faith grows exceedingly, and the love of every one of you all abounds toward each other" (2 Thessalonians 1:3). "Exceedingly growing faith" means you should be able to act quickly on the word, when the prompt comes, to issues of life. Whenever something comes against you as a believer, you should be able to act faster than you did in earlier years. "Exceedingly growing faith" implies that you should be getting to the point where you are instantly faith-sensitive (to Rhema) in every situation where acting in faith is called upon.

Many word-knowledgeable Christians have slowed down in complacency when it comes to operating in faith. They are no longer hot, but kind of lukewarm. When negative or undesirable circumstances of life come against them, they become furious, and react like the world acts, cursing, getting upset, nervous, worried, and popping pills. This is indeed worrisome.

Proverbs 3:5-6 says, 'Trust in the Lord with all your heart, And lean not on your own understanding. In all your ways acknowledge Him, And He shall direct your paths." To trust anything or anyone other than the Lord results in disaster (Proverbs 11:28; Ezekiel 16:15). To lean on something in "trust" is to use as if it were a crutch (2 Samuel 1:16, Job 8:14-15). Understanding is good only if it is from the Lord (Proverbs 9:10). To acknowledge God in all ways is to invite His presence into all daily activities. To "direct" is literally make straight or smooth, and God will make righteousness attainable. We should stop trying to make God's word to work, but start acting on the word.

The important point in any situation is to find out what God's word has said about the subject. We need to always be certain in our mind and know that the word is true, and act as though it is true. This is the time it becomes a reality in our lives. Consequently, we become mighty in our prayer life when we get an understanding to always harmonize a confession of our hearts with a confession of our lips.

We need to always demonstrate that we know that the word is true! To get the reward of our healing as believers, for example, we must be convinced in our soul and spirit and act out our belief in the truth of God's word; that Bible teachings or divine teachings are created to impress it upon our heart that Jesus indeed still heals today.

We eventually get transformed into an energetic and victorious life in God's service without symptoms if we recognize real faith as a fruit of the knowledge of God's word. We must also act upon it like it is true, instead of trying to rationalize to believe it.

FAITH GROWS THROUGH KNOWLEDGE

Many Christians have been long in church without a corresponding increase in faith in manifestation of godly manners and divine responsibilities. This is simply because they have no knowledge of the things of God. They may know a great deal about denominational matters, but lack knowledge of spiritual matters.

Romans 10:13-14 says, "For "whoever calls on the name of the Lord shall be saved." How then shall they call on Him in whom they have not believed? And how shall they believe in Him of whom they have not heard? And how shall they hear without a preacher?"

Paul cited biblical support for the universal offer of salvation. The promise is for all who call on the name of the Lord. Jesus is Lord – that is Yahweh ("Lord" in Joel 2:32). Proverbs 23:23 states, "Buy the truth, and do not sell it, Also wisdom and instruction and understanding." This admonishes believers to seek the knowledge and understanding of the truth and stick to it.

Romans 10:17 says, "So then faith comes by hearing, and hearing by the word of God." Despite that many Christians have been church members for a very long time, they are still not Bible-oriented and not grown in deeper knowledge of the divine order in the Kingdom. If your faith is not growing, it is a reflection that your understanding of the word is not growing either. Real faith is certainly the product of knowledge and understanding of the word of God. Faith originates directly in God's word, and it always has a direct relationship with God's word.

Jesus says in John 6:63, "It is the Spirit who gives life; the flesh profits nothing. The words that I speak to you are spirit, and they are life." Human reason cannot discern spiritual truth without being aided by the Spirit. The Jews wrongly believed that studying the scripture (John 5:39) and doing *"works of the law"* (John 6:27-29) were sufficient for spiritual understanding. But they erred. The only way to get faith is through the word.

Lack of knowledge and understanding of God's word is a hindrance and reason for doubt and unbelief. This deficiency will also hinder and hold believers in bondage since they, consequently, cannot appropriate God's promises beyond actual knowledge of God's word. The ultimate way to receive revelation knowledge of God is through reading, meditation upon the word, and constantly hearing the word being preached. If you take time to feed upon the word of God and constantly benefit from the ministry gifts that God has set in the church, such as the ministry gift of teaching, then you will be fully liberated, and life will come to reside in your spirit.

Apostle Paul exhorts in Ephesians 4:17-19, "This I say, therefore, and testify in the Lord, that you should no longer walk as the rest of the Gentiles walk, in the futility of their mind, having their understanding darkened, being alienated from the life of God, because of the ignorance that is in them, because of the blindness of their heart; who, being past feeling, have given themselves over to lewdness, to work all uncleanness with greediness."

God said His people went into captivity and were destroyed because they lacked understanding, and did not have knowledge (Hosea 4:6). Today, the case is not too different. Many church-going people are held in captivity by evil habits such as sex violations, drugs, alcohol, prejudice, and all other types of evil captivities. If they had knowledge of the promises about our redemptive rights in God, they would not pollute their bodies with all kinds of filthy habits emanating from lusts for worldly affairs. A lack of knowledge about the truth and what God's word says results in doubts, unbelief, ignorance of our redemption, as well as of our rights in Christ Jesus.

FIGHTING THE GOOD FIGHT OF FAITH

Apostle Paul admonishes us in 1 Timothy 6:11-12, "But you, O man of God, flee these things and pursue righteousness, godliness, faith, love, patience, gentleness. Fight the good fight of faith, lay hold on eternal life, to which you were also called and have confessed the good confession in the presence of many witnesses." Fleeing sin is paired with a vigorous pursuit of virtue, which corresponds with eternal life. The fight is not against any church or denominational group. And it is important that we fight because it is God's intent and purpose for us to surely win! Believers are predestined to be victorious always.

Real faith is the product of the word available as a weapon of warfare for Christians to win the battle of life. 1 John 5:4-5 states, "For whatever is born of

God overcomes the world. And this is the victory that has overcome the world—our faith. Who is he who overcomes the world, but he who believes that Jesus is the Son of God?" People who are "born of God" are those who have been transformed and made new through faith. A lack of knowledge will hinder and hold believers in bondage – that is, in the narrow place of failure and weakness - because they cannot appropriate the promises of God beyond the actual knowledge of God's word. Hallelujah! We do not need to fight sin as Jesus Christ has already put sin away permanently once and for all by sacrificing Himself (Hebrews 9:16).

RIGHTEOUSNESS BY FAITH

God inputted righteousness into those in the Old Testament (OT) whose sins have been covered by the blood of bulls and goats. But in the New Testament (NT) we become righteous new creatures. Romans 1:17 says, "For in it the righteousness of God is revealed from faith to faith; as it is written, "The just shall live by faith.""

God's righteousness was the core of Paul's message. God's righteousness can be understood in several ways. First, God always does what is right and can be said to have righteousness as one of His attributes

(Deuteronomy 32:4; Psalm 119:142). Second, since God does what is right, His actions or activities are sometimes identified as His righteousness (Isaiah 45:8; 46:13; 51:5-6; 56:1).

Third, God's righteousness is a gift from Him to us, justifying us in His sight. "Justification" – the righteousness of God - is that righteousness which he imparts in order to make men righteous. In the gospels, God reveals His righteousness (His nature and His gift of right status) by faith. Apostle Paul explained how God is able to declare sinners to be righteous because of Jesus' work on the cross. "From faith to faith" emphasizes that the entire process of being declared righteous comes from start to finish by faith.

We are the righteousness of God in Him, and as God's righteousness, we receive the bountiful fullness of God. A lack of understanding of our righteousness – what it is and what it gives to the believer - holds more people in bondage than anything else in our Christian walk. When we are finally able to fully realize that we are the righteousness of God, then we step out of the narrow place of failure and weakness in which we have lived into the boundless fullness of God, Hallelujah!

Hebrews 11:6 also reveals, "But without faith it is impossible to please Him, for he who comes to God must believe that He is, and that He is a rewarder of those who diligently seek Him." Other results of faith are declaration of righteousness, the ability to understand that faith is possible only because God is faithful, the ability to accomplish great things in the world, and the ability to see that even when believers are persecuted and murdered, beyond this world is a better resurrection. It is a fundamental truth for believers to know that no one can please God without faith!

Romans 8:1-2 declares, "There is therefore now no condemnation to those who are in Christ Jesus, who do not walk according to the flesh, but according to the Spirit. For the law of the Spirit of life in Christ Jesus has made me free from the law of sin and death." Believers are set free from indwelling sin because there is no more condemnation, no more under the law; they have been released from the law (Romans 7:6).

The believer's freedom comes from Jesus' incarnation and sacrifice for sin, and by the Holy Spirit's operation in providing life. The Son, the second person in Trinity, took on humanity. He did not cease to be God but took on a real human nature (without sin) and became the perfect offering. He fulfilled the law's demands in His life and in His death and broke sin's power in the flesh on the cross.

Faith is essential and all-important, and Christians need to be people of strong faith. We must put on the armor of God and fight the good fight of fight. It is equally important to always make positive declarations, decrees, and professions, as well as acting promptly to the unction of the Holy Spirit in response to all circumstances of life.

CHAPTER 10

TAKE TIME TO BE HOLY

Take time to be holy, the world rushes on;
Spend much time in secret, with Jesus alone.
By looking to Jesus, like Him thou shalt be;
Thy friends in thy conduct His likeness shall see.

—William D. Longstaff

Observation reveals that there is a general misunderstanding of the concept of living holy. "Holiness" is often misconstrued by many believers to be something so difficult, boring, and even undesirable. They are aware of the truth that God commands His children to be holy and may even desire to obey Him, but the lusts of the present life get into their way of thinking and prevent them from seeing the true picture and benefits of holiness.

WINNING VIRTUES

The world misunderstands the believer trying to live right and condemns him by alleging that he considers himself better than other people. Sometimes, Christians want to please the Lord and live a godly life, but they end up being accused of having a "holier-than-thou" attitude toward others around.

The other extreme involves mimicking the physical appearance of people or objects to portray the state of being in true "holiness". For instance, there are some Christian sects and denominations who wear peculiar clothes, forbid makeup and jewelry, and comb their hair in a particular way or simply refuse to comb it. They generally try to look plain, dull, unattractive, and think that makes them look holier than others.

Some churches promote "standards", such as dress codes, and set rules to be obeyed by their members, and those who often come to church. Don't get me wrong - godly standards are pretty good; but they are often taken to the extreme and are substituted for honest Christian moral standards.

On a lighter note, another extreme situation is when we think of someone being "holy" and our mind instantly envisions a monk in a cloister, with a shaved head, beanie cap, long brown ropes, and with a suffering look on his face. Yet another extreme is the idea that a person who is holy walks around all day, making religious statements, chanting, glowing with a halo above their heads, and totally different in appearance and disposition from other people.

Let me share a "joking blast" I received recently from a fellow church member on a Sunday morning between the church parking lot and the sanctuary. Apparently, the said member parked his car next to my car, just a moment after I had left the parking lot. He tried to catch up with me on the pathway to the sanctuary for the Sunday service as he cracked the joke. I happen to drive a white truck, a capsule-shaped 450 GL Mercedes Benz SUV. This guy tried to articulate "holiness" in his imagination as he told me "Hey, your truck in the lot is really holy, trying to worship like us!" I laughed and chuckled as we entered the sanctuary.

Due to lack of knowledge and understanding of the word, some churches, even the sincere ones, have misinterpreted Romans 12:2. They think that, since the Lord has told us not to be conformed to the world, then wearing a particular attire, wearing no shoes, or having a certain pious look and appearance makes one holy. This is not true.

While I was teaching a Sunday School class recently on a Sunday morning at RCCG, Living Word Chapel, in Houston, Texas, I was suddenly distracted by a lady who entered the front door, wearing a cap over a beautiful "Nigerian" attire, which appeared absurd for such a beautiful native dress. My mind went straight to her denomination back in Nigeria, West Africa, where they maintained such a dress code.

I was able to identify the sect as they are well noted, males and females, for wearing an "all-white" attire, including long robes, to the ankle; brown ropes, white cap, and no shoes! Sorry to say, but they usually appear totally out of place anywhere outside of their premises. Let me repeat: One does not become holy by looking in a certain way or dressing up outward appearance or even actions.

All these extreme scenarios can be likened to the case of a monk who claims to be living a strict of life following Jesus. As such, he breaks fellowship with the world, begins to live in isolation, then claims martyrdom, because no one likes him anyway. Believers and Christians must avoid projecting this kind of picture to the world as the typical life in the Kingdom.

MEANING OF HOLINESS

The Webster's Dictionary defines holy as follows: "Dedicated to religious use; belonging to or coming from God; spiritually perfect or pure; untainted by evil or sin; sinless; sanity". "Sacred" refers to that which is set apart or holy or is dedicated to some exalted purpose. To be separated means to be consecrated to God. In the Old Testament many things are called holy, such as:

- Ground
- Convocation
- Habitation
- Sabbath
- Nation
- Men
- Places
- Gifts
- Garments
- Anointing oil, etc.

It should be noted that these things were not holy in themselves; they became holy when they were dedicated and set apart for service unto the Lord.

What, for instance, made the Ark of Covenant holy? The gold in it was holy once it was placed in the tabernacle and dedicated to God. It had no moral qualities. In plain terms, it was the same as it was before in the ground, except that it had now been refined and used in the service of the Lord. It was totally separated for the service for the Lord. It could no longer be used in any other way and for nothing else. This can also be applied to other consecrated objects and individuals. Let's explore this in detail.

WHAT HOLINESS ENTAILS

1. Attitude of the heart is the issue. First and foremost believers must correct the wrong notion that holiness has to do with the outward appearance. 1 Samuel 16:7 says, "But the Lord said to Samuel, "Do not look at his appearance or at his physical stature, because I have refused him. For the Lord does not see as man sees; for man looks at the outward appearance, but the Lord looks at the heart."

Eliab had a favorable appearance and stature, which Samuel had found admirable, but God knew him to be unworthy. So, we must understand that being holy means to be totally dedicated to the Lord. Believers will certainly seek and pursue to do what is necessary to truly make the commitment to live for the Lord. The believer's commitment to the Lord will direct how he lives his life. The true Christian will be self-disciplined and conduct himself as God's instrument and will keep clear and free from sin.

Biblical holiness is the state and issue of the heart, separated in a totally unwavering devotion to God, which controls the believer's life and directs him to abstain from even the appearance of evil (1 Thessalonians 5:22).

2. Gird up the loins of your mind. Ephesians 6:14-15 states, "Stand therefore, having girded your waist with truth, having put on the breastplate of righteousness, and having shod your feet with the preparation of the gospel of peace." Paul calls believers to put on the whole armor of God, which points to its divine nature more than its completeness. Standing with your loins gird about with truth means to prepare your mind for action. You must desire and make up your mind that you are going to do what the Lord wants because He wants the best for you. You must also set your hope fully on the grace the Lord has given you.

Believers must stop conforming their desires after the evil desires they had while they were still in their former state of darkness. Many Christians struggle with the issue of holiness because they have never made the decision to once and for all deal with sin, and live for the Lord. In our Christian lives, we are to be prepared and recognize the possibility of falling into sin and becoming unfaithful. This is the same reason people are trained in advance to deal with certain emergencies. For example, we maintain fire extinguishers, and practice or have fire drills in homes, schools, and places of employment, to get ready and prepared in case of the eventuality of fire incident. In this way, you know already how to react in the moment of danger.

Believers should not be complacent to think they are above sin and failing the Lord, which can really make them prime candidates for a fall. Apostle Paul, in Romans 12:3, says, "For I say, through the grace given to me, to everyone who is among you, not to think of himself more highly than he ought to think, but to think soberly, as God has dealt to each one a measure of faith." As part of a renewed mind, the Christian is to think wisely about himself and what his function is to be in the body of Christ (1 Corinthians 12:12-28). "Measure of faith" means that a person should measure himself by God's word only, and not the dictates of men or the world.

3. Present your body as a living sacrifice. Romans 12:1-2 says, "I beseech you therefore, brethren, by the mercies of God, that you present your bodies a living sacrifice, holy, acceptable to God, which is your reasonable service. And do not be conformed to this world, but be transformed by the renewing of your mind, that you may prove what is that good and acceptable and perfect will of God."

Believers are to present their bodies as a living, holy and acceptable sacrifice unto God. This principle is presented in both negative and positive versions; be not conformed to the world (negative), be ye transformed or changed (positive); by renewing your mind (positive).

2 Peter 3:17 also states, "You therefore, beloved, since you know this beforehand, beware lest you also fall from your own steadfastness, being led away with the error of the wicked." Those who think themselves as having attained holiness are sometimes the least holy as they really have to work on achieving it rigorously and systematically. Usually, the person who thinks they have "arrived" in their Christian life (over-confident), probably has never even taken off.

BENEFITS OF HOLINESS

The following are the reasons we must take time to be holy:

1. Intimacy with God. Holiness activates intimacy with God, and consequently builds spiritual strength, confidence and stability in the believer. Hallelujah! Such is the huge divine reward for the character of those who may dwell with the Lord, as fully revealed in Psalm 15:1-5: "Lord, who may abide in Your tabernacle? Who may dwell in Your holy hill?

He who walks uprightly, and works righteousness, and speaks the truth in his heart; He who does not backbite with his tongue, nor does evil to his neighbor, nor does he take up a reproach against his friend;

In whose eyes a vile person is despised, but he honors those who fear the Lord; He who swears to his own hurt and does not change; He who does not put out his money at usury, nor does he take a bribe against the innocent. He who does these things shall never be moved."

God's "tabernacle" is paralleled to His "holy hill", and refers to the sanctuary of Yahweh. This is the place of God's presence and protection (Psalm 61:4). Certain people are not allowed in God's presence because of His holiness, but the desire of God's people is to be in His presence forever (Psalm 65:4; 84:3-4). "Walks uprightly" refers to a life of integrity. The truth of God is not due to mere proclamation, but must reside in a person's heart, which is the mind or the inner person (Deuteronomy 6:6; Isaiah 29:13). God is intolerant of those who maliciously destroy others with their speech (Psalm 101:5).

We must love what God loves, and hate what He hates. Despising the wicked and honoring the godly are attitudes that show we are made in God's image. Believers should never profit in monetary terms from someone else's misfortune or lack (Proverbs 15:27). Those who are able to enter God's sanctuary will be secure (Psalm 16: 56-60), and will never be moved.

2. Usefulness and effectiveness for God's purposes. Holiness makes believers vibrant, effective, and very useful for God's divine purposes. This is revealed in 2 Timothy 2:20-26; "But in a great house there are not only vessels of gold and silver, but also of wood and clay, some for honor and some for dishonor. Therefore if anyone cleanses himself from the latter, he will be a vessel for honor, sanctified and useful for the Master, prepared for every good work. Flee also youthful lusts; but pursue righteousness, faith, love, peace with those who call on the Lord out of a pure heart. But avoid foolish and ignorant disputes, knowing that they generate strife. And a servant of the Lord must not quarrel but be gentle to all, able to teach, patient, in humility correcting those who are in opposition, if God perhaps will grant them repentance, so that they may know the truth, and that they may come to their senses and escape the snare of the devil, having been taken captive by him to do his will." Lusts refer to sinful desires that are characteristics of youth such as immoral sexual desires, longing for novelty, or impulsiveness. To know the truth is gateway to salvation. Paul describes humanity as enslaved by the devil and in dire need of rescue (2 Corinthians 4:4).

3. Abundant fruit-bearing. Holiness pleases God and produces "fruit", particularly love and wisdom. Ephesians 5:1-17 says, "Therefore be imitators of God as dear children. And walk in love, as Christ also has loved us and given Himself for us, an offering and a sacrifice to God for a sweet-smelling aroma…See then that you walk circumspectly, not as fools but as wise, redeeming the time, because the days are evil. Therefore do not be unwise, but understand what the will of the Lord is." Believers are urged to learn about Christ (Ephesians 4:20-21), and not to grieve the Spirit (Ephesians 4:30). While they cannot imitate God in power, knowledge, or presence, but they can imitate Him is self-sacrifice and in manifesting a forgiving spirit (Ephesians 4:32).

4. Holiness causes people to glorify God. Holiness makes people around you to readily identify and appreciate God's glory in your life. 1 Peter 3:10-18 states, "For "He who would love life and see good days, let him refrain his tongue from evil, and his lips from speaking deceit. Let him turn away from evil and do good; let him seek peace and pursue it. For the eyes of the Lord are on the righteous, And His ears are open to their prayers; But the face of the Lord is against those who do evil. And who is he who will harm you if you become followers of what is good? But even if you should suffer for righteousness' sake, you are blessed...For Christ also suffered once for sins, the just for the unjust, that He might bring us to God, being put to death in the flesh but made alive by the Spirit." Believers are commanded to distinguish themselves by doing good, even when faced with pagan hostility, because God will vindicate the righteous.

5. Holiness builds peace with God. 2 Peter 3: 10-18 says, "But the day of the Lord will come as a thief in the night, in which the heavens will pass away with a great noise, and the elements will melt with fervent heat; both the earth and the works that are in it will be burned up....You therefore, beloved, since you know this beforehand, beware lest you also fall from your own steadfastness, being led away with the error of the wicked; but grow in the grace and knowledge of our Lord and Savior Jesus Christ. To Him be the glory both now and forever. Amen."

God's patience towards sinners is not inexhaustible. The day of the Lord will be sudden and will catch many people unprepared, as when a burglar sneaks in and robs a house (Matthew 24:43-44; Luke 12:39-40). The anticipation of the Lord's return and its accompanying events of judgement should rouse Christians to holy living. Evil will be completely destroyed when Christ returns, and righteousness will permanently dwell in the new heavens and a new earth (Isaiah 32:16). This will usher in the peace of God's reign.

6. Holiness blocks Satan's inroads into our lives. If you are living in sin, you allow the devil to bring death and destruction into your life. Yielding to holiness is yielding to God, the author of that holiness that produces godly results. Romans 6:15-16 warns, "What then? Shall we sin because we are not under law but under grace? Certainly not! Do you not know that to whom you present yourselves slaves to obey, you are that one's slaves whom you obey, whether of sin leading to death, or of obedience leading to righteousness?" This is the process of freeing believers from being slaves of sin to becoming slaves of God. Sin is no longer the believer's ruler, since sin gained its power by using the law, but the Christian is under the rule of grace. Apostle Paul also asserted in another extended analogy that people have a choice about which master they will serve. Whoever you serve and obey thrusts you under his power and control. Sin pays a wage to his subjects – death; while obedience to God brings righteousness and the gift of eternal life.

YOU CAN BE HOLY

For the born-again believer, living holy is a fruit – not root - of salvation. It is a by-product of having a right relationship with God, but not a means to obtain it. This is a powerful revelation for us! We need to always search deep into the Scripture, which is the everlasting power of God unto salvation.

God provided believers everything needed as a free gift through Christ's death, burial, and resurrection. We must appreciate and thank God for His grace, setting us free from guilt, condemnation, and a performance-mentality. Our motive for living holy is not to get God to accept us, since our right standing with God is based on His grace, not our performance.

Holiness is about putting our faith in Christ Jesus. We must determine to live holy because God commands it, and it is our nature to live that way, and thereby not give the devil access into our lives.

CHAPTER 11
DOMINION OVER SICKNESS

Daily living by faith on Christ is what makes the difference between the sickly and the healthy Christian, between the defeated and the victorious saint. —A.W. Pink

---

Believers have the exclusive privilege to choose to live above sickness and ultimately live in divine health all the days of our lives. After all, God's desire for us, according to 3 John 2, is to "prosper in all things and be in health, just as your soul prospers."

Good health is valued in every age, but in ancient times, it was even more valued, since medical care could be ineffective and life expectancy was low. It is vital to be fully aware that sickness and disease don't just pounce on anyone out of the blues; they usually give you notice by "knocking on the door" with some signals. The way you respond to these signals will determine whether they eventually settle or not.

EMPOWERED FOR VICTORY

Believers are already equipped spiritually by God with all that they need to resist the signals and tricks of infirmities. 2 Timothy 1:7 says, "For God has not given us a spirit of fear, but of power and of love and of a sound mind." "Spirit" refers to the Holy Spirit; and boldness, not cowardice, is a mark of the Holy Spirit (Proverbs 28:1; Acts 4:31).

When you start feeling not so right, that's a wake-up call for you to firmly resist sickness or diseases by attacking them and not allowing them to settle or overtake you and your activities. You must never wait or postpone action for either sin or sickness to overtake you before you firmly react and war against them. You need and must inflict that aggressiveness against it straightaway. You must immediately free yourself from indwelling sin, and set yourself free.

Romans 8:2-3 says, "For the law of the Spirit of life in Christ Jesus has made me free from the law of sin and death. For what the law could not do in that it was weak through the flesh, God did by sending His own Son in the likeness of sinful flesh, on account of sin: He condemned sin in the flesh." The believer's freedom comes from Jesus' death and resurrection, and by the Holy Spirit's operation in providing life. You don't have to get sick or allow sin or sickness to overtake you. Jesus has done it once and for all times. You can get healed all the time, stay in health, and needing no healing. This is the heritage of believers, as prescribed by Christ! Hallelujah!

Believers should meditate on entire Psalm 91, and thus be fortified against all infirmities while enjoying absolute victory. Psalm 91:10-11 says, "No evil shall befall you, nor shall any plague come near your dwelling; for He shall give His angels charge over you, to keep you in all your ways." The word "plague" (infection, attack or epidemic) reinforces the concept of serious physical threats (Leviticus 13:2; 14:3, 32, 54). The Lord's angels serve as His messengers and agents of His power outside the sanctuary (Psalm 103:20; Genesis 24:7; Hebrews 1:14). They have superior power, including the ability to protect the Lord's people from harm (Genesis 19:10-11; 24:40; Isaiah 63:9; Daniel 3:28).

ACTIVATING YOUR VICTORY OVER SICKNESS

1. Frame your mind to always abide in the presence of God. The believer's mind is a powerful divine tool that is able to sense and see sickness. The question is, can you also see demons? If you don't settle it in your mind that you are impenetrable, that these things cannot come upon you, then you are at a delicate risk, and you will be vulnerable to infirmities. However, believers should never ever allow infirmities to harass them.

There is safety in abiding in the presence of God. Psalm 91:1-2 says, "He who dwells in the secret place of the Most High shall abide under the shadow of the Almighty. I will say of the Lord, "He is my refuge and my fortress; My God, in Him I will trust." 2 Corinthians 5:17 also states, "Therefore, if anyone is in Christ, he is a new creation, old things have passed away; behold, all things have become new."

As a born-again Christian and believer, you are seated in a new place in God that is far above all sicknesses and diseases, as well as powers and principalities. The words "in Christ" refer to being in union with Him, while genuine conversion begins with life transformation, not by reforming the old nature. The indwelling Spirit creates the divine life in believers (Romans 8:8-10), enabling life of new. In the New Testament, other passages communicate this truth by using expressions such as "regeneration" or "born-again".

2. Make no room for the devil. Your body is the temple of God – thus, there should be no room for the devil or sickness. 1 Corinthians 6:19-20 says, "Or do you not know that your body is the temple of the Holy Spirit who is in you, whom you have from God, and you are not your own? For you were bought at a price; therefore glorify God in your body and in your spirit, which are God's."

The believer must consciously war against sin, tendencies and ailments that tend to assault the sanctity of a believer's sacred oneness with Christ (sealed by the Holy Spirit who is in you) and the oneness of holy matrimony (1 Corinthians 7:2). The believer's body is a sacred vessel, bought at a price by the Son of God. Believers thus have no business doing anything, including carelessness, with the Lord's body that does not glorify Him.

Ephesians 4:27 says, *"...Give no opportunity to the devil."* (ESV) A similar counsel is contained in James 4:7, "Therefore submit to God. Resist the devil and he will flee from you." To "submit to God" involves the idea of self-humbling and being sensitive to evil works of sin and disease, while "resist the devil" suggests an active resistance against threats and temptations. The believer has a very vital role to play in the entire process of systematic resistance against sickness and sin and all ungodly activities.

3. Surround yourself with like-minded encouragers. As a believer, it is important that you surround yourself with like-minded people who will encourage you more positively on the path of righteousness, faith and sound health, rather than people who will weaken you with vicious or negative tales. Proverbs 13:20 says, "He who walks with wise men will be wise, but the companion of fools will be destroyed." Associating with the wise will make you wiser, but being a companion of fools will make you vulnerable to the destruction of foolish counsel.

Hebrews 10:24 says, "And let us consider one another in order to stir up love and good works." Believers are encouraged to rather stir or provoke one another to good works that are physically, spiritually, and emotionally beneficial to the fellowship. Proverbs 27:17 says, "As iron sharpens iron, so a man sharpens the countenance of his friend." Just as a man sharpens an axe or a carving knife, good friends encourage one another to grow in wisdom and godliness, even if it requires painful criticism out of love, but an enemy gives kisses (Proverbs 27:26) with deceit in mind. Resist them.

Also, don't hang out with people who ask you to yield to or nurse sickness or disease because "it is God's will". Completely do away with people who always narrate negative stories, expecting and speaking evil. Maintain your distance; be protective over your space and individual atmosphere. Never give room to overbearing friends who usually come up with discouraging scenarios. It is very vital to fellowship with like-minded people, that are truly "born-again", that believe the Holy Bible.

4. Quench all fiery darts by faith. Ephesians 6:16 states, "above all, taking the shield of faith with which you will be able to quench all the fiery darts of the wicked one." This involves the "whole armor of God" which Apostle Paul urges believers to put on (Ephesians 6:13). With the shield of faith (manifested in your actions and declarations), you can repel every symptom of infirmity, every negative diagnosis, as well as every prevailing ailment in your locality.

BELIEVERS' AUTHORITY TO LIVE IN DIVINE HEALTH

The ministry of our Lord Jesus Christ on earth was preoccupied with compassion for the people, while He went about doing good, and healing a great multitude of people. Matthew 4:23 states, "And Jesus went about all Galilee, teaching in their synagogues, preaching the gospel of the kingdom, and healing all kinds of sickness and all kinds of disease among the people." "All kinds" implies that no type of ailment was beyond Jesus' power to heal.

Similarly, while sending out His twelve disciples, Jesus commissioned them (and all believers) to go and do greater works – including healing the multitudes of all manner of sicknesses and diseases. He says in Matthew 10:7-8, "And as you go, preach, saying, The kingdom of heaven is at hand.' Heal the sick, cleanse the lepers, raise the dead, cast out demons. Freely you have received, freely give."

Mark 11: 22-24 states, "So Jesus answered and said to them, "Have faith in God. For assuredly, I say to you, whoever says to this mountain, 'Be removed and be cast into the sea,' and does not doubt in his heart, but believes that those things he says will be done, he will have whatever he says. Therefore I say to you, whatever things you ask when you pray, believe that you receive them, and you will have them." Jesus gave His confirmation on His promises about faith and impossibilities to settle in our minds about maintenance of strong, unshakeable faith.

DECREES AND DECLARATIONS ON DIVINE HEALING

The following are some of the prayer points, declarations and Bible truths that can be used to activate the promises of God on divine health and healing by believers. As Romans 8:2 states, "For the law of the Spirit of life in Christ Jesus has made me free from the law of sin and death."

- No evil befall me nor any will any plague come near my dwelling – Psalm 91:10-11

- I will not be sick - by His stripes I am healed – Isaiah 53:5

- The spirit of Him who raised Jesus from the dead dwells in me. He who raised Christ from the dead will also give life to my mortal body – Romans 8:11

- Sin will never reign in my mortal body, I rebuke obedience to lusts – Romans 6:12

- I am healed by Christ's stripes – 1 Peter 2:24

- I receive the balm of Gilead for my healing – Jeremiah 8:22

- I am healed by prayers of faith – Jeremiah 5:16

- The Lord has heard my prayers and I am healed – Jeremiah 17:14

RIGHTEOUSNESS AND HEALING: THE CONNECTION

The believer's healing authority is inherent and solely hangs on our spiritual identity. The gift of healing is part of the Sovereign God's love and a built-in potential into every believer. However, our spiritual identity becomes manifest when we are established in righteousness. We do not receive the gift of spiritual healing from heaven; it is activated only when we are established in righteousness - which is a gift from God – and not earned by works or any other means.

Isaiah 54:13-15 states, "All your children shall be taught by the Lord, and great shall be the peace of your children. In righteousness you shall be established; You shall be far from oppression, for you shall not fear; And from terror, for it shall not come near you. Indeed they shall surely assemble, but not because of Me. Whoever assembles against you shall fall for your sake."

In a sequential order, righteousness goes in front and ahead of the believer (being established as a gift of God by grace), and this will be backed by the glory of God (signs and wonders) following us all the days of our lives. This will eventually activate the gift of healing.

The believer manifests his spiritual identity, while he walks in Christ's righteousness which activates healing miracle. This must involve a display of boldness, emanating from revelation of our joint-heir relationship with Christ. The glory of God shall back you up as your rear guard.

Isaiah 58:8-9 says, "Then your light shall break forth like the morning, your healing shall spring forth speedily, and your righteousness shall go before you; The glory of the Lord shall be your rear guard. Then you shall call, and the Lord will answer; You shall cry, and He will say, 'Here I am.'" Righteousness goes ahead of us, while the glory of God backs us up as we maintain our spiritual identity with Him in Christ's righteousness. We derive our boldness from the revelation of our joint son-ship with Christ.

Romans 5:14-17 states, "Nevertheless death reigned from Adam to Moses, even over those who had not sinned according to the likeness of the transgression of Adam, who is a type of Him who was to come… For if by the one man's offense death reigned through the one, much more those who receive abundance of grace and of the gift of righteousness will reign in life through the One, Jesus Christ.)"

The works of Adam and Jesus have a similar scope but drastically different effects. One's offense plunged humanity into ruin, but God gave the Gift that brought justification, in spite of many sins. What was gained through Jesus is far greater than that which was lost through Adam.

2 Corinthians 5:17-21 relates how believers became reconciled to God. We are new creatures and the indwelling Spirit creates a divine life in us (Romans 8:8-10), enabling a life of new things. The believer

need not wait for the gift of healing from heaven since he has already gotten the gift of righteousness through Christ by grace. Hallelujah!

However, Hebrews 5:13 warns against spiritual immaturity. The believer must grow spiritually for all imputed virtues to manifest the fullness of God's power.

Here are some key points to note once again:

- Healing miracle falls out of the gift of righteousness

- You don't need the gift of healing to heal; it is activated by the gift of righteousness.

- Christ's imputed righteousness is a gift of God and not of works.

- You need the REVELATION of the word of righteousness.

- You cannot grow in righteousness because it is a gift of God (which is Christ's righteousness).

- Always remind yourself of Christ's righteousness input; identify with it to boost your boldness to deliver healing.

GO FORTH AND HEAL!

You need to be conscious that God has already deposited all you need to heal people inside you as a believer. You are His ambassador and under command to use His power to heal. He made you righteous by giving you the free gift of righteousness by grace, not your works. You are just under His command to heal by laying your hand on the sick. All you need to do is ACTIVATE Jesus' healing power being conveyed through you as a believer in Jesus Christ who gave you the free gift of righteousness which eventually activates the gift of healing.

So, friend, all you have to do is just lay your hand on the sick and pronounce "Be healed in Jesus' name!" or "Receive your healing in Jesus' name!" PERIOD. If you know the ailment, you may add, "I rebuke you (name of disease) in Jesus' name." That is all you have to do with BOLDNESS, since it is in Jesus' name.

I have been successfully demonstrating this healing authority since the last 18 years. I started by getting my healing from rheumatoid arthritis. I recently used this process to heal my most recent grandson, here in Houston, Texas. He had a cold symptom, with a nagging cough, which I rebuked, and then pronounced his healing in Jesus' name. It is amazing how this healing process worked instantly. Hallelujah!

WINNING VIRTUES

I pray and hope you will always remember to lay your hand to heal all manner of infirmities, and perform more wonders than our Lord Jesus according to His command.

CHAPTER 12

FINDING TRUE HAPPINESS

The key to lasting happiness and real pleasure in this world is not found in seeking gratification, but in pleasing God. And while the Lord desires that we enjoy His gifts and the people to whom we are joined, He wants us to know that we were created first for His pleasure. —Francis Frangipane

The world's way of seeing happiness is in agreement with its dictionary definition – a mental state of well-being, characterized by positive or pleasant emotions, ranging from contentment to intense joy. The dictionary definition of happiness presents a picture of happiness as a state of mind that is dependent on fleeting circumstances and situations.

In reality, the old adage is very true - if we count our blessings one by one, we will be pleasantly surprised by how many favors and miracles that God has wrought in our lives. However, most of God's great blessings to people in the world seem to be transient because they only experience and display happiness, while the memory of the blessings lasts. The worldly people's appetites are not easily satisfied; they always want more blessings from God without giving back in appreciation.

Mental and emotional depression has become frequent among even the elites, as demonstrated by frequent suicide committed by rich celebrities, and famous millionaires. Apparently, all their material wealth could not buy them peace and happiness.

END-TIME TREND

One of the signs of the end-times is ingratitude, particularly when people have acquired a lot of wealth and later focus their attention on power and money. Romans 1:21 says, "Because, although they knew God, they did not glorify Him as God, nor were thankful, but became futile in their thoughts, and their foolish hearts were darkened."

Because of human willfulness, people's knowledge of God became clouded and their thinking became darkened. Without contact with God, the center of man loses contact with reality, misses the purpose of his existence, and ultimately becomes ungrateful.

People are supposed to glorify God as the Almighty, but instead find all sorts of created objects to worship, including money and power. Part of the wrath of God is revealed in humanity's loss of intelligent musing. This also causes lack of satisfaction with excessive material acquisitions; as well as lack of peace of God, resulting in aggression to others, and suicidal inclinations.

Assuming that we Christians are to live according to the entirety of the dictionary definition of happiness, then we would, like the rest of the world, be people just hanging delicately on a thread of life that has no deep meaning or substance to it. Thank God, however, that our case is different.

Happiness and its secret to the believer can be found in the following ways:

1. Joy: This is the wholesome, unspeakable, exceeding, indwelling, flowing effervescent and complete experience of a believer in Christ. The world can't comprehend it, and does not have it. 1 Peter 4:13 says, "But rejoice to the extent that you partake of Christ's sufferings, that when His glory is revealed, you may also be glad with exceeding joy."

Believers are to rejoice in the test that suffering brings for being members of God's household. Suffering for Christ in this world characterizes believers as strangers, with heaven as their future place of eternal residence.

Jesus, in John 15:11, states, "These things I have spoken to you, that My joy may remain in you, and that your joy may be full." This was spoken to establish the process of love and joy perfected in the believer. Obedience is not all gloom and doom; rather, it's a source of joy.

The Old Testament prophets envisioned a period of great end-time rejoicing (Isaiah 25:9; 35:10; 61:10; 66:10; Zechariah 9:9). While narrating the parable of the talents, Jesus says in Matthew 25:21, "His lord said to him, 'Well done, good and faithful servant; you were faithful over a few things, I will make you ruler over many things. Enter into the joy of your lord." The faithful servants (true disciples) used their gifts and resources responsibly and were generously rewarded. The wicked and lazy servant (a false disciple) failed to use the resources and was severely punished.

2. Peace: An infectious happiness radiates through us as believers and elevates us when the peace from above surrounds our hearts. This peace, which surpasses all understanding, elevates us beyond the realm of the natural. Like joy, the peace that comes from the Holy Spirit, defies the natural sphere of life, and consequently makes us strong in the inner man.

Christ, in John 14:26-27, says, "But the Helper, the Holy Spirit, whom the Father will send in My name, He will teach you all things, and bring to your remembrance all things that I said to you. Peace I leave with you, My peace I give to you; not as the world gives do I give to you. Let not your heart be troubled, neither let it be afraid."

The expression, "peace" (shalom), is used both as a greeting and to announce the blessing upon those who enjoy a right relationship with God (Numbers 6:24-26; Psalm 29:11; Haggai 2:9). The Old Testament prophesied a period of peace following the Messiah's coming, for He is the Prince of Peace (Isaiah 9:6). There would be tidings of peace and salvation (Isaiah 52:7; 54:13; 57:19), and God would establish an everlasting covenant of peace with His people (Ezekiel 37:26).

Jesus' parting encouragement for His followers not to be troubled or afraid echoes Moses' parting counsel (Deuteronomy 31:6, 8). Philippians 4:6-7 states, "Be anxious for nothing, but in everything by prayer and supplication, with thanksgiving, let your requests be made known to God; and the peace of God, which surpasses all understanding, will guard your hearts and minds through Christ Jesus."

The peace of God brings power to endure. The peace calms a troubling situation when explanations fail. Furthermore, peace guards by keeping anxieties from hearts (choices) and minds (attitudes).

3. Trust and dependence on the Holy Spirit: Believers are told by the book of Proverbs not to lean on our understanding, strengths, or weaknesses. When we are not leaning on all these self-aggrandizements, we are able to attain happiness by just realizing that God will never leave nor forsake us. Proverbs 3:5-6 states, "Trust in the Lord with all your heart, and lean not on your own understanding; In all your ways acknowledge Him, And He shall direct your paths."

To trust anything or anyone other that the Lord results in disaster (Proverbs 11:28; 28:26, Psalm 52:7; 62:10; Isaiah 30:12; Ezekiel 16:15). Understanding is pretty good (Proverbs 16:16), but only if it is from the Lord. To acknowledge God in all one's ways is to invite His presence into all daily activities and decisions. Direct is literally "make straight" or "smooth" while God will make righteousness attainable. 2 Corinthians 12:9-10 states, "And He said to me, "My grace is sufficient for you, for My strength is made perfect in weakness." Therefore most gladly I will rather boast in my infirmities, that the power of Christ may rest upon me. Therefore I take pleasure in infirmities, in reproaches, in needs, in persecutions, in distresses, for Christ's sake. For when I am weak, then I am strong."

The sufficiency of divine grace may be easier to grasp intellectually than through experience. God ensured that Paul never got away from grace. God's glorious power is more evident when it is displayed in weak vessels.

4. Spiritual deliverance: Happiness can be attained from spiritual deliverance through the leading of the Holy Spirit. Moving in the realm of the Spirit is not a mental exercise. If we could follow the Spirit of God and the word of God, without human reasoning getting in the way, we would be better off! God doesn't operate through man's mind - because it hasn't been born again; rather, He operates through the recreated spirit of man.

If the Holy Spirit doesn't choose to manifest Himself in spiritual gift, it is advisable to keep teaching people how to stand against sickness and disease with the word of God. The word always works. For example, Isaiah 53:5 says, "…And by His stripes we are healed." Romans 8:11 also states, "But if the Spirit of Him who raised Jesus from the dead dwells in you, He who raised Christ from the dead will also give life to your mortal bodies through His Spirit who dwells in you."

The Spirit's presence is the mark of Christ's ownership and the Spirit provides life and righteousness. The leading of the Spirit of God is His providential sanctification (Psalm 23:3). It is the Spirit's empowerment for mortification of fleshly desires (Romans 8:13). Romans 8:2 also says, "For the law of the Spirit of life in Christ Jesus has made me free from the law of sin and death."

The believer's freedom comes from Jesus' incarnation and sacrifice for sin, and by the Holy Spirit's operation in providing life. By constantly and rigorously reading and meditating over these scriptures, the believer can get desired deliverance, and consequently attain eternal joy and happiness.

Faith and obedience count with God; and it is rewarding to follow the leading of the Holy Spirit and do what He directs you to do. The Holy Spirit will always lead you in line and in tune with God's word. So, always anticipate the Holy Spirit to give you direction on what to do.

It is vital to learn and teach people the word, and let God do the rest. God will surely make His word good in people's lives if they will dare to stand by it. Of course, if people don't stand by God's word, He doesn't have anything to make good in their lives. It is wise to build your life and ministry on the word; then you will experience its manifestations.

The word of God is the power of God unto salvation, deliverance, healing, and victory! The word of God did it all and there is indeed power in the word. It is important for Christians to be taught the word effectively, and to encourage them to put the power of God to work for them by believing and trusting God's word. They must declare and decree the word, as well as acting on it as if it is true.

Being a believer, you are seated with Christ in the heavenly places, far above principalities and powers. Jesus' victory over the devil is your victory because you are in Him. No demon can deter you. Your sitting with Christ in heavenly places signifies a position of authority, honor, and triumph – not failure, depression, bondage and defeat. Hallelujah!!!

5. Contentment: This is a state of wellbeing that is not determined by physical or material possessions. It is a state of being satisfied and happy with whatever condition one finds oneself at any point in time. As Paul testifies of his own experience, "Not that I speak in regard to need, for I have learned in whatever state I am, to be content: I know how to be abased, and I know how to abound. Everywhere and in all things I have learned both to be full and to be hungry, both to abound and to suffer need." (Philippians 4:11-12).

The word "learned" implies a lesson resulting in better knowledge, while "content" means self-reliance or self-sufficiency that grows out of trust in Christ. "I know" results from evaluating various circumstances, both difficult and good. The New International Version renders the passage thus, "I am not saying this because

I am in need, for I have learned to be content whatever the circumstances. I know what it is to be in need, and I know what it is to have plenty. I have learned the secret of being content in any and every situation, whether well fed or hungry, whether living in plenty or in want."

1 Timothy 6:6-10 also states, "Now godliness with contentment is great gain. For we brought nothing into this world, and it is certain we can carry nothing out. And having food and clothing, with these we shall be content. But those who desire to be rich fall into temptation and a snare, and into many foolish and harmful lusts which drown men in destruction and perdition. For the love of money is a root of all kinds of evil, for which some have strayed from the faith in their greediness, and pierced themselves through with many sorrows."

Note that what is condemned here is "harmful lusts", not the possession of things. The warning is not simply that love of money can be harmful, but that this craving has led some people to deny the faith and show themselves to be unbelievers.

6. The righteousness of God: Believers are the righteousness of God through faith by grace. The righteousness that we have is one that is inputted in us through our relationship with Christ. God's righteousness through faith is expressed in Romans 3:22-24, which says, "even the righteousness of God, through faith in Jesus Christ, to all and on all who believe. For there is no difference; for all have sinned and fall short of the glory of God, being justified freely by His grace through the redemption that is in Christ Jesus."

Jesus is the object of our faith and the means of obtaining the gift of the righteousness of God. The gift is for both the Jews and the Gentiles who believe. All have missed the mark that God intended for the human race and have lost the glory of the original creation (Psalm 8:5). Believing the Good News starts the process of the restoration of glory (Romans 8:30; 2 Corinthians 3:18).

"Justified" means that Christians are declared to be righteous (Romans 5:1, 9; 8:30; 1 Corinthians 1:30; 6:11). The judge deems believers innocent because of Jesus' work on the cross. "Freely" means that God grants justification, not due to any merit in Christians but solely by His grace, the undeserved love and mercy of God.

"Redemption" is a commercial term that refers to purchasing freedom for slaves or military prisoners. The purchase price for our freedom was the blood of Jesus Christ (Mark 10:45; 1 Peter 1:18-19). The mere fact that God looked at unworthy people like us and declared us righteous through the finished work on Calvary is a major source and secret of happiness in Christ.

King David celebrates the same truth, as Romans 4:5-6 states, "But to him who does not work but believes on Him who justifies the ungodly, his faith is accounted for righteousness, just as David also describes the blessedness of the man to whom God imputes righteousness apart from works." David, Israel's greatest king, sang about the blessedness that God gave him in the forgiveness of his deliberate sins. David understood that, in God's accounting ledger, his sins were wiped out and righteousness was inscribed in their place.

7. Unity: "United we stand, divided we fall", so goes the popular saying. We individually gain profound happiness when we are standing together as one body of Christ, either in the family or in the corporate body. A spiritually and physically healthy environment creates a happy life for all brethren in that association or body of Christians. But when there is so much rancor and strife, the spirit of moodiness thrives, which is ungodly. Acts 2:46-27 says, "So continuing daily with one accord in the temple, and breaking bread from house to house, they ate their food with gladness and simplicity of heart, praising God and having favor with all the people. And the Lord added to the church daily those who were being saved."

Early Christian gatherings took place in two places - the temple and the homes of the believers. The early church was an evangelizing church, growing daily. Evangelism appeared to have taken place primarily through the gathering of Christians in the temple and homes. The crucifixion and resurrection of Christ were at the heart of early Christian preaching which called for immediate response from anyone who listened.

8. Being a pleasure to God: A believer can receive happiness coming from God in the form of a gift to those who do things that please Him and glorify His name. Ecclesiastes 2:26 states, "For God gives wisdom and knowledge and joy to a man who is good in His sight; but to the sinner He gives the work of gathering and collecting, that he may give to him who is good before God. This also is vanity and grasping for the wind."

Ecclesiastes is preoccupied with how death nullifies all man's accomplishments. It emphasizes that our days under the sun are limited, and thus it is a tragedy to waste those days with excessive labor and grief. There are obviously many more things to a good life than just drinking and eating, and enjoying one's work. It is not a suggestion for us to abandon ourselves to pleasure-seeking or our careers, but we ought to recognize the reality that life is short and not miss out on its basic pleasures. These, too, are gifts of God and sure ways through which happiness can come to us from Him.

YOU CAN HAVE LASTING HAPPINESS!

Note that the secret of happiness for the believer is not founded on physical, material or educational achievements. While these things are good, as long as you relish them, they only make you feel good at the moment you have them; you may abruptly revert to sadness as soon as you lose them. By the time you really discover what true happiness as outlined in this chapter means, you will realize the truth that you don't FEEL good - you LIVE good!

Believers are created in the image of God Almighty – so, they cannot be bipolar or subject to change. Romans 11:28-9 says, "Concerning the gospel they are enemies for your sake, but concerning the election they are beloved for the sake of the fathers. For the gifts and the calling of God are irrevocable."

We must continue to live in the consciousness of the full nature of God in us. As we do, happiness will remain our eternal possession. Depression, with all its associated evil agents, will never come near us or our abode. They will never know our names in the MIGHTY name of Jesus! Amen.

CONCLUDING NOTES

This book is meant to usher you into a new life that manifests fully in the four inherent virtues that are crucial to our Christian walk. These fundamental virtues include wisdom, courage, temperance and justice (Philippians 4:8). Courage is most essential in a believer's life to combat life's challenges, particularly as we fight the fight of good faith for eternal life, and to win and discover God's purpose for our lives.

A believer must persevere and be always patient, while maintaining a high level of loyalty and integrity to find rest in a restless word. The believer must be furnished thoroughly with the word of God, and totally be separated for use by God, by living a life of holiness. Above all, we must be courageous in tackling all challenges of life to connect with God's gift of victory and eternal happiness which He pre-destined for our lives.

Be determined not to quit. Quitters are losers, but those who persevere will surely win in the end!

ABOUT AYORINDE IDOWU

Ayorinde Idowu is currently a serving Minister at RCCG, Living Word Chapel, Houston, Texas USA. He completed an intensive formal ministerial training at the Whole Life Success Ministry Institute (WLSMI) in Houston, Texas and has since been a Sunday School Coordinator at RCCG.

He earlier retired from an active professional career as Chief Geologist/Geophysicist after 25 years in the petroleum industry. He is currently a Science Lecturer at the University of Houston-Downtown (UH-D), and an Adjunct Faculty Geology Professor at Houston Community College (HCC) respectively.

REFERENCES

BOOKS

Reinhard Bonke, Holy Spirit: Are We Flammable or Fireproof? Published by Christ for all Nations, 2017

Finis Jennings Dake: God's Plan for Man – Revealing God's Plan for all Creation, Dake Publishing Inc., 2010

Gary Oates with Robert Paul Lamb: Vision & Dreams, Recognizing God's Supernatural Signs, Open Heavens Publications, 2004

Dr. A. L. Gill: Destined for Dominion, Powerhouse Publishing 1992, Fawnskin, CA 92333

Dr. A. L. Joyce Gill: Supernatural Living Through the Gifts of the Holy spirit, Powerhouse Publishing, 1995

Holman Study Bible NKJV Edition, 2015, Comprehensive Study Notes, Essays, Articles, and Full Color Maps

Bill Johnson: Hosting the Presence – Unveiling Heavens Agenda, Destiny Image Publishers Inc, 2012

Kenneth E. Hagin: The Triumphant Church – Dominion Over All Powers of Darkness, 1993

ESSAYS & ARTICLES

RCCG Living Word Chapel (LWC) Bible Study Notes, Year 2004 to Date

Kenneth E. Hagin: Hops Prayer: Six Enemies to Faith, 2004

Rick Warren: Be in Constant Communion with God, 2014

Andrew Womack: Staying Full of God

http://www.sermoncentral.com/sermons

The Lie of Insignificance

http://www.glowlifeaslight.com/2015/06/the-lie-of-insignificance

Communion with God – What?; Why?; and How? 2013

http://www.desireinggod/blog/posts

How you can be an Overcomer, Church of God International. 2018

http://cgi.org/how-you-can-b-an-overcomr/

Thomas W. Finley, The Victorious Life: A Lesson Series for the Earnest Christian, 2002

http://seekersofchrist.org/VCL/VCL - less11.html

Rebecca Greenwood, Destined to Rule: Spiritual Strategies for Advancing the Kingdom for God, Baker Publishing Group

http://bakerpublishing group.com/book/destined-to-rule/282740

Rebecca Greenwood, Walk in Dominion – Charisma Magazine

https://ww.charismag.com/spirit/spiritual-warfare/2425-take-up-your-scepter

Harold Herring, 7 Steps To become a Kingdom Conqueror And a World Overcomer

https://harold herring.com/blogs/richthoughts/6057-steps-to-become-a-kingdom...

John Piper, the absolute Sovereignty of God: What Is Romans None About?

http://www.desiringgod.org/messages/the-absolute-sovereignty of god

Shawn Shoemaker: 4 Characteristics of an Overcomer, Apostolic Life http://www.apostoliclife.org/4-characteristics-of-an-overcomer/

In Constant Communion With God: Vincentia Ministries, Kenya, 2018

http://vincentianministerieskenya.org/blog/in-contant-communion-with...

www.ingramcontent.com/pod-product-compliance
Lightning Source LLC
Chambersburg PA
CBHW070753100426
42742CB00012B/2114